# WHO'S WHO IN THE HISTORY
## OF PHILOSOPHY

# WHO'S WHO
# IN THE
# HISTORY OF PHILOSOPHY

by

THOMAS KIERNAN

*PHILOSOPHICAL LIBRARY*

*New York*

# PREFACE

The principal aim of this book is a modest and severely practical one — to provide students as well as anyone else more than casually interested in philosophy and its history with a quick, concise and easily accessible source of reference. That the book might be read in its entirety, with pleasure and profit, is a secondary aim. In either case, its principal features are an intentional directness of language and a rather broad generalization of concept for the purpose of rendering — briefly, clearly and in outline — the fundamental philosophic views of each thinker included.

The requirement of brevity has often meant bold and unqualified statements or descriptions, but these can be counted as an advantage since the ultimate design of the book is to acquaint rather than instruct the reader. It is my hope that by such a means of acquaintance with philosophy and philosophers the reader will feel compelled to further explore this at once most blessed and exasperating of intellectual disciplines.

It goes without saying that the limitations imposed by its very nature upon a book of this kind demand some sort of public recognition, if not apology, on the part of the author. However, although the limitations of the book are indeed narrow, I believe that within its stated framework it performs a meaningful function and satisfies — assuming that it is competently executed — a definite need.

The book's format is simple enough. In composing it, I have followed three general rules: (1) That the entries should be listed in alphabetical order — for purposes of reference, this order has more to recommend it than a chronological order, which is better suited to a different type of survey of philosophy.

(2) That each entry should contain some biographical data including, with dates, the more important events in the life of each philosopher. (3) That each entry should present, in the simplest language possible, a concise exposition or representation of the principal points in the philosophy of the particular thinker covered by the entry.

In regard to this last point, I can only apologize for any errors of interpretation. Most of the philosophers surveyed in these pages, along with their philosophies, have been the objects of hundreds or thousands of critical volumes written over the centuries, all of which endeavor in one way or another to interpret, explain and refine. It would be patently presumptuous of me to imagine myself an authority on the thought of any philosopher, no less to claim myself capable of distilling and extracting the essence of that thought in a paragraph or two. Yet, for the purposes of this book, that is exactly what had to be attempted. I can only hope, therefore, that my brief and sometimes cryptic sketches of each philosopher's central theories and doctrines satisfy the requirements of the book by focusing on the salient and most relevant points of that philosopher's thought.

For the sake of facilitating the use of this volume, and in line with achieving brevity and simplicity of expression, I have taken advantage of certain typographical devices. At the head of each alphabetically listed entry, the philosopher's name is printed in **bold face.** When I feel that the reader, while studying the description of a particular philosopher, might benefit further by consulting the description of another philosopher to whom the subject of the entry might have been philosophically related, I indicate this cross-reference by having the other philosopher's name printed in SMALL CAPITALS. In addition, words or phrases printed in *italics* in the text of any entry are done so in order to impress upon the reader the specific category or school of thought to which the particular philosopher subscribed, or to indicate a notable doctrine or theory he might have advanced.

As a concluding word, I might mention that my criterion for the inclusion or omission of any philosopher was almost exclusively based on whether or not I felt the philosopher had made an original, or at least co-original, contribution to the history of philosophical ideas. The entire philosophic tradition, from pre-Socratic days to the present, can be effectively described as a connective progression of ideas or concepts, each growing out of the preceding and each influencing the following. I would narrow this down even further to ideas or concepts having to do with the most vital and traditional concerns of philosophy — the nature of reality, the nature of being, the nature of existence, and the nature of thought. So then, it is those who have had a hand, whether in a major or minor fashion, in advancing the primary concerns of philosophy that I have chosen to include.

Thomas Kiernan

New York

# WHO'S WHO IN THE HISTORY
## OF PHILOSOPHY

# A

**Abelard, Peter** (1079-1142). Born at Pallet, France, he died at Cluny. A brilliant thinker and teacher, he became an important figure in the Church, yet was condemned for heresy (1121) and later censured by the Council of Sens (1141).

He set the course of medieval philosophy for two centuries with his interest in the problem of universals. His fundamental conclusion was that universals are not real and have no existence — they are merely words. Basically, then, he was a *nominalist*.

Chief works: *Sic et Non* (*Yes and No,* c. 1122); *Theologia Christiana* (c. 1124); *Scito Teipsum* (1125-38). His personal life has been celebrated in literature.

**Abravanel, Don Isaac** (1437-1508). Born in Lisbon, he later emigrated to Spain. However, being a Jew, he was expelled by the Spanish Inquisition and settled in Italy. Died at Venice. He wrote many philosophical works, but was mainly known as an interpreter of MAIMONIDES. Key work: *The Forms of Elements* (1557).

**Abravanel, Judah** (1470-1530). Son of DON ISAAC ABRAVANEL. Wrote *Dialoghi d'Amore,* a dialogue in the fashion of those of PLATO, in which "love" is postulated as the principle of the universe — love emanates from God to beings, and from beings returns to God. (He was also known as Leone Ebreo.)

1

**Adamson, Robert** (1852-1902). Scottish thinker born at Edinburgh, he specialized in the study of the philosophy of KANT and later developed his own doctrine, which he called *critical realism* (i.e. universals are as real as, if not more real than, the realm of objective existence and can be known through the mind). He was for many years a professor of philosophy and logic at the Univ. of Glasgow. Key works: *On the Philosophy of Kant* (1879); *The Development of Modern Philosophy* (1903).

**Adler, Felix** (1851-1933). Born at Alzey, Germany, he was brought to the U. S. at the age of 6. He founded the American Ethical Union and the Society for Ethical Culture. His philosophy maintained that the idea of a personal God is unnecessary; that the social and ethical behavior of man constitutes the Godhead; and that man's personality, because of its unique and inviolable nature, is the force to which religion should be devoted. Chief works: *Creed and Deed* (1878); *Moral Instruction of Children* (1892); *An Ethical Philosophy of Life* (1918).

**Aenesidemus** (c. 100 B. C.). A native of Crete, he lived and taught at Alexandria, Egypt, and was a philosopher of *relativism* and *skepticism*. He held that man has no way of understanding the true nature of the universe or God, and that man's conceptions about these are *relative*. No two views are alike because no two men are alike; hence, there can be no *single* truth understood by man.

**Ailly, Pierre d'** (1350-1420). Theologian, philosopher and scientist, he was born at Compiègne, France, and became a cardinal of the Church and Chancellor of the Univ. of Paris. His philosophy distinguished between rational knowledge and intuitive knowledge. He claimed that it is *intuition* that permits man to be certain of the primary objects of consciousness (being and non-being). From this, he developed a *theory of probability* for the existence of God, using a doctrine of *verisimilitude* (i.e. if we can be sure of the existence of material objects, then we can be *probably* sure of the existence of such things as ideas and spiritual things relating to these objects, since it is probable that such ideas have existence from their similarity to objects to which they relate. Thus, because we have an objective idea of God, it is probable that He exists). Key works: *Questions on the First, Third, and Fourth Senses; On the Soul.*

**Alain de Lille** (c. 1128-1202). French Scholastic philosopher, he was born at Lille and died at Citeaux. He was an eclectic who tried to temper the rational with the mystical. He held that the mind unaided by revelation can know the universe, but only through faith can man know God. He was known as the "Universal Doctor."

**Albertus Magnus** (1206-1280). Born at Lauingen, Bavaria, as the Count of Bollstädt, he became a Dominican priest (1223). A liberal and encyclopedic thinker, he was called "Doctor Universalis". He taught THOMAS AQUINAS; he later became Bishop of Ratisbon (1260) and an important figure in the Church. He did much to popularize a great part of Aristotelian and Arabic philosophical thought in the 13th century. His own system was a vast synthesis of diverse schools of thought that preceded him. He believed not that the world was actually created by God, but that creation proceeded from God according to a necessary order, without the specific act of creation. He propounded other views that were similar to this in that they sought to give a rational, philosophical base to Catholic dogma. Chief works: *Summa de Creaturis* (1245-50); *Summa Theologiae* (1270). All Albertus' works were published in 38 volumes in Paris (1890-99).

**Albo, Joseph** (1380-1444). Spanish-Jewish medieval philosopher who is important to the philosophy of religion for his famous

3

defense of Jewish doctrine at Tortosa, Spain (1413). He established the criteria whereby the primary and fundamental doctrines of Judaism may be distinguished from those doctrines of secondary importance. Key work: *On Fundamental Principles* (1425).

**Alcott, Amos Bronson** (1799-1888). American philosopher-teacher who was born at Wolcott, Conn., and died at Concord, Mass. A contemporary of EMERSON, he was one of the famous *transcendentalists* who dwelt on the spiritual, as against the material, aspects of life. Key work: *Spiritual Culture* (1841).

**Alexander of Hales** (c. 1190-1245). A Franciscan teacher and Scholastic philosopher whose importance derives from the fact that he created a philosophical system which served as a model for those members of the Church who mixed faith with reason. He was called the "Irrefragable Doctor" because his arguments were held to be unassailable. Much of his teaching set the style for the later Scholastic philosophy of AQUINAS and others. Major work: *Summa Universa Theologiae.*

**Alexander, Samuel** (1859-1938). Born at Sidney, Australia, he became a notable thinker and teacher in England. His fame rests mainly on his book *Space, Time and Deity* (1920), often referred to as the most significant British contribution to metaphysics since that of HOBBES.

He made the process of *emergence* a metaphysical principle (i.e. all things are forever in a process of emergence). He identified *Space-Time* as the indivisible principle of all things, and claimed that matter and motion were the mediative elements between *Space-Time* and the objective world; all things that exist (e.g. material things, life, mind, etc.), exist because they *emerge* from *Space-Time* through the interaction of matter and motion. Classed as both a realist and an idealist, he tended toward *realism* as he grew older.

4

**Al Farabi** (c. 870-950). Born near Farab in Turkey, he introduced Aristotelian logic into the world of Islam and was known to posterity as the second Aristotle. His principal philosophical concern was with the soul, and he did much to explore and refine the divisions of philosophy that ARISTOTLE had set out.

**Al Gazali** (1058-1111). Persian thinker whose works to this day are considered classics in the Moslem world. He subscribed to the doctrine of *emanation* derived from neo-Platonic writings. Although he used philosophy, he felt it was meaningful only as an introduction to theology. Main works: *Destruction of Philosophy; Religious Renovation*.

**Al Kindi** (c. 815-873). The first of the important Arabian followers of Aristotle, he was born near Basra and died in Bagdad. He was primarily a mathematician, but made significant contributions to the theories of knowledge and being. His view of knowledge was stated in terms of *dualism* (i.e. there are two intellects, *active* and *passive;* knowledge occurs when the passive intellect is activated by the active intellect). His metaphysics recognized five primary substances — matter, form, motion, place and time — from whose interaction the universe is caused.

**Ambrose** (c. 340-397). Born at Trèves, France, he was second only to AUGUSTINE in helping to lay the philosophical foundation for the Catholic church. As Bishop of Milan, he introduced the idea of separating Church and state.

**Anaxagoras** (c. 500-428 B. C.). Renowned as the last of the great Ionian philosophers, he taught Thucydides, Euripides and other noted Greeks, and was the first philosopher to choose Athens as his home. He was also the first to introduce the *teleological argument* in explaining the universe (i.e. since the universe displays a design and order, there must neces-

5

sarily be an *eternal principle* behind the design; therefore, the world cannot have formed by accident). From this, he proceeded to develop an *atomic* theory of reality which held that all things are composed of infinitely minute particles (atoms); these particles, by their motion and coming together, combine into a variety of material objects that are kept moving in an orderly sequence of time and arrangement of space through the guidance of the *eternal principle* (known to the Greeks as *nous*). This theory was later refined by DEMOCRITUS and others, and has had an important influence throughout philosophy.

**Anaximander** (c. 611-546 B. C.). Along with THALES and ANAXIMENES, he formed the *Milesian* school of Greek philosophy. He explained the numerous processes of nature as emanating from a single principle, or *world-stuff;* he thus helped to develop the concept of *the infinite* as the source of the universe: the universe developed from infinity by means of rotation. Key work: *On Nature* (a fragment).

**Anaximenes** (c. 550-480 B. C.). One of the three leaders of the *Milesian* school of Greek philosophy. His importance is due to his formulation of the theory whereby change is represented as the result of the processes of condensation and rarefication (which anticipated the discoveries of some of the laws of physics). In this theory was embedded his notion of the first principle of the universe: *air* (all things derive from air). Where his co-thinker THALES had postulated all things as developing out of *water,* and where ANAXIMANDER had said that the *infinite* was the source of all things, Anaximenes combined the qualities of each and concluded that only *air,* being the basic element in the universe, had those qualities which would allow it to be characterized as the *infinite.*

**Anselm** (1033-1109). Born at Aosta, Italy, he became a Benedictine monk (1060) and subsequently was appointed

Archbishop of Canterbury (1093). His general philosophy was based on that of AUGUSTINE and was largely oriented toward a justification of Roman Catholic dogma.

He is most noteworthy for his invention of the much discussed *ontological argument* for the proof of the existence of God (i.e. we all understand God as that than which our thought can conceive of nothing greater; since something which is the greatest but does not exist must, by logic, be less great than something which is the greatest and also exists, the former cannot really be the greater; the greatest, therefore, has to exist, and because we understand nothing as being greater than God, God must exist). Key works: *Proslogium; On Truth.*

**Antisthenes** (c. 444-365 B. C.). Born of an Athenian family, he was founder of the *Cynic* school of Greek philosophy. (It should be noted that cynic philosophy is in no way related to the modern meaning of cynicism, but derives its name from the *Cynosarges,* the building in Athens in which ANTISTHENES taught). He was a faithful student of SOCRATES and was present at the latter's death. He was a philosophical opponent of PLATO and took pleasure in ridiculing the latter's doctrine of Ideas: "I am able to see the horse, but I cannot see its horse-ness," he once wrote. His main concern was with virtue and practical philosophy, and he felt, in line with his cynicism, that since man is essentially alone in the world (i.e. without laws to guide him), he must live in society according to his own laws.

**Aquinas, Thomas** (1225-1274). The leading philosopher of the Roman Catholic Church, his authority was officially established by Pope Leo XIII (1879). He was born near Naples, the son of the Count of Aquino. After an early religious education at the Benedictine monastery at Monte Cassino, he decided to become a Dominican priest. Toward this end he studied first at the Univ. of Naples (1239-1244), then at the Univ. of Paris under ALBERTUS MAGNUS (1245-

1248). After four years of further study at Cologne, he returned to Paris and was awarded the *licentiae docendi* in theology (1256). He taught at the Papal Curia (1259-1268), returned to Paris to put down the growing tide of Averröism (1269-1272), and finally returned to the Univ. of Naples where he taught for two more years. He died while on his way to the Council of Lyons (March 7, 1274).

Aquinas subordinated philosophy to theology, natural law to the revelation of Christ, and human society to the dogma of the Church. His importance to philosophy has a threefold derivation: (1) He demonstrated the dependence of AUGUSTINE's thought on PLATO and at the same time pointed out that Augustine found many limitations in Platonism, inferring from this that Augustine did not have the credentials to be considered the author of the highly elaborate and sophisticated Platonism later expounded by AVICEBRON (Ibn Gabirol) in his *Fons Vitae* and by AVICENNA in his commentaries on the metaphysics of ARISTOTLE; (2) In bringing this out, Aquinas concerned himself with analyzing the Platonic inspiration of the various interpreters of Aristotle and with separating what was to him the authentic Aristotle from the aberrations brought about by his Platonic interpreters — in this sense, the philosophical activity of Aquinas can be best appreciated as a systematic critique and elimination of Platonism from the medieval interpretation of Aristotle's metaphysics, psychology and epistemology; (3) The result of this detailed critique is known as the *Aristotelian-Thomistic Synthesis,* indicating Aquinas' success in re-directing Aristotelian philosophy towards truth and away from doubt, towards belief and away from scepticism. Ultimately, Aquinas used this synthesis to support and defend the doctrines of Christianity, and he proved to the satisfaction of many that faith was not incompatible with reason. Major works: *De Ente et Essentia* (1256); *Summa Contra Gentiles* (1260); *Summa Theologica* (1267-73); various commentaries on Aristotle's works.

**Arcesilaus** (315-241 B. C.). Greek philosopher who succeeded CRATES as the head of the Platonic Academy (268 B. C.). He advocated a philosophy of *skepticism* and felt that suspended judgment was the best approach in attempting to attain truth.

**Archelaus.** A disciple of ANAXAGORAS, he belonged to the *Sophist* school of Greek philosophy. His attention was directed primarily to ethical problems; he especially distinguished between man's natural impulses and the dictates of moral law, and felt that natural impulse was much the better guide to proper conduct.

**Ardigo, Roberto** (1828-1920). A leader of the Positivist movement in Italian philosophy. Born at Padua and educated as a Catholic priest, he subsequently became interested in the views of COMTE. He eventually abandoned the priesthood and became a professor at the Univ. of Padua. His emphasis on the importance of psychology in the human scheme of things eventually differentiated his thought from that of Comte. Chief works: *Psychology as a Positivist Science* (1870); *The Morality of the Positivists* (1885).

**Aristarchus** (c. 315-265 B. C.). Born on the island of Samos, he was a Greek astronomer whose importance to speculative philosophy lay in his theory (which preceded that of COPERNICUS by almost 2000 years) that the sun is the center of the universe and that the earth travels around it in an oblique orbit. Because the implications of this theory would have negated the importance of man in the universe, it was not generally accepted by philosophers.

**Aristippus** (c. 435-356 B. C.). Sometimes he was referred to as Aristippus of Cyrene. He was originally a *sophist,* then, SOCRATES' disciple, and finally the founder of the *Cyrenaic* school of Greek philosophy. He taught that *pleasure,* under-

9

stood as the sensation of gentle character, was the true end of life; to him, all pleasures were equal in value but differed in degree and duration. Unlike Socrates, he denied social responsibility and was not too impressed with the potential of man's reason, except insofar as it could control his indulgence in pleasure.

**Aristotle** (384-322 B. C.). Born in the Greek colony of Stagira in Macedonia, at 18 he became a student of PLATO at Athens and remained for nearly 20 years as a member of the Platonic Academy. After Plato's death, he left Athens and, among other things, became the tutor of young Alexander of Macedonia, later known as Alexander the Great. Eventually he returned to Athens (335) where he spent 12 years as head of a school he set up in the Lyceum (known as the Peripatetic School). As the result of an outbreak of anti-Macedonian feelings in Athens after the death of Alexander (323), he was forced to leave the city for Chalcis, where he died a year later.

Aristotle possessed one of the few truly encyclopedic minds in the history of western man. Those of his works which still exist cover all the sciences known to his time and are characterized by subtlety of analysis, sober and dispassionate judgment, and a superior mastery of facts and evidence — collectively, they constitute one of the most monumental achievements ever credited to a single mind.

He divided the sciences into the *theoretical,* the aim of which was objective knowledge; the *practical,* the aim of which was the guidance of conduct; and the *productive,* whose aim was the guidance of the arts. He put above and before these three divisions the science and art of logic — called by him *analytics* — its mastery the requisite to all other investigations, since its purpose was to set forth the conditions to be observed by all thinking that had truth as its aim. Beginning with this principle, he spent his lifetime ferreting out the truths of all the sciences, from ethics

10

to art, from physics to politics. He was the originator of the syllogism (that form of reasoning whereby, given two propositions, a third follows necessarily from them by nature of a term common to both premises — e.g. all men have brains; Jack is a man; therefore, Jack has a brain) which is the core of deductive logic.

At the heart of his complex philosophy is his concept of *dualism* — the duality of all things in the universe — a concept he initiated and which has had an unalterable influence on the course of philosophy ever since. Everything is made of a union of *matter* and *form,* he postulated, and the two are interdependent, one incapable of existing without the other. The matter of an object is what makes it an object; the form is what makes an object the particular thing it is (table, man, etc.). The two together constitute the *being* of an object (matter possessing the capacity for form, form requiring matter to define its being). Aristotle developed this philosophy primarily to refute PLATO's doctrine that being belongs only to the universal Ideas of things (the Forms) and cannot exist in the material manifestations of these Ideas (in other words, the being of a chair or tree is not in the particular chair or tree, but in the universal Idea of the chair or tree, for each object is but a single, imperfect manifestation of a singular, perfect Idea).

To support and complement his doctrine of the *dualism of being,* Aristotle also developed a corresponding dualism of *potentiality* and *actuality*: matter is the *potentiality* of any object, while form is that which gives the object its *actuality*. With these twin distinctions in hand, he claimed to have solved the difficulties that earlier thinkers had encountered in attempting to explain the process of *change,* visible in everything about them. Change, according to Aristotle, is the process by which matter becomes form, by which potentiality becomes actuality (and not the passage from *non-being* to *being,* as previous thinkers had considered change to be). He called this process *entelechy.*

11

The system of nature as thus developed by Aristotle consists of a series of matter-and-form existences on many levels, in which the forms of simpler beings act as the matter for the next higher beings, and so on. Hence, at the base of nature is *prime matter* which, having no form, is mere potentiality and not actual being. The simplest formed matter are the primary elements — earth, air, fire, water. These, in their forms, constitute the matter for the next in the line of ascending forms; and these forms comprise the matter for the next higher, etc., until man is reached, the highest of the universe's beings. Man's reason is the highest of the forms, and is what gives him actuality as man and defines him; whereas God, existing, so to speak, at the opposite end of the spectrum from prime matter, is pure form. These basic principles, formulated by Aristotle in his *Analytics,* were carried into all the diverse studies he undertook and helped to solve the problems raised by each inquiry. He explained all questions in the light of his conclusions in logic and applied these conclusions with equal effectiveness to, among other things, problems about time and space, God, human good, the state, and the arts. Although modern science has rendered much of Aristotle's thought obsolete, he is still a force in modern thought; further, a very large part of our technical vocabulary, both in science and philosophy, is rooted in the terms Aristotle used and defined. Among his works: *Prior Analytics; Posterior Analytics; Physics; On The Heavens; On the Soul; Metaphysics; Nicomachean Ethics; Politics; Rhetoric; Poetry.*

**Arnauld, Antoine** (1612-1694). Born in Paris, he is remembered as the most forceful leader of the doctrine of *Jansenism* (a doctrine which held that if human nature is totally corrupted by original sin, man, because of this corruption, is equally unable to resist both fleshly desires and grace; therefore, he must lack free will). This doctrine was strongly condemned by the Church and caused a great deal of controversy in philosophy in its time. Key work: *Treatise on True and False Ideas* (1683).

**Augustine** (354-430). Born Aurelius Augustinus at Tagaste, near Carthage, in North Africa, he was the son of a pagan father and a pious Christian mother (Monica, who herself achieved sainthood). He embraced Christianity in his early 30's, though he had been an adherent of skepticism and Manicheism (a doctrine that sought to fuse Buddhist, Zoroastrian and Christian beliefs into a single, acceptable faith). He was ordained shortly after his conversion, became Bishop of Hippo (North Africa) at 41, and filled this office until his death.

His works deal with the problems of divine omnipotence, predestination, God, the Trinity, and creation. Although concerned principally with matters of religious doctrine, Augustine revealed himself as a poetic metaphysician in his analysis of fundamental principles, and although his conclusions might be classified as highly motivated, he gave the Church a philosophy of ethics and metaphysics as well as a monumental philosophy of history. In his work *The City of God* (413-26), he enunciated the famous doctrine of the *four epochs* of human history, a doctrine that was impressed upon the consciousness of Western civilization until the time that HEGEL's dialectic and COMTE's positivistic approaches shed new light on the possibilities of history. It is not the originality of his ideas so much as the profundity of his psychological analysis that makes Augustine a great figure in the history of philosophy. His autobiographical *Confessions* (400) has been regarded for many centuries as a model of self-analysis. His influence was especially marked on Luther, PASCAL, DESCARTES and LEIBNIZ.

*Illuminism* is the term most used to describe the idea at the heart of his philosophy. In his metaphysics he used the concept of *illumination* to define the manner in which being is properly perceived (all beings are illuminated ontologically,

**13**

i.e. they have their own illumination from within — from their ontological components, such as number, unity and order). A highly mystical philosophy, to be sure, but counter-balanced by a Platonic emphasis on forms and ideas, with God as the ultimate idea from which all being derives.

**Aurelius, Marcus** (121-181). Roman thinker and statesman who subscribed to the basic tenets of *stoicism* and also became Emperor of Rome (161). His philosophy is best known through his work *Meditations,* in which he advocates peace of soul and perpetuates the two fundamental doctrines of *stoicism*: the autonomy of the individual and his indepen-dence of the universe. Key work: *Meditations.*

**Aurobindo, Sri** (1872-1950). Indian philosopher and mystic born in Bengal. Educated in England, he returned to India and became involved in political life until he left for the French colony of Pondichéry to devote himself to study and con-templation. His philosophy centers in his doctrine that the existence of the Absolute is manifested in *pure reason.* He therefore advocated purification of the mind through con-templation as the way of raising it to the level of pure reason and the Absolute. Key work: *The Life Divine* (1942).

**Avenarius, Richard** (1843-1896). A German philosopher, he was born in Paris. He expressed his thought in an elaborate and novel terminology in the hope of constructing a symbolic language for philosophy that would protect philosophical thought from the corruption of opinion and assumption.

He formulated the doctrine of *empirio-criticism* (knowl-edge should consist of statements that are merely descriptive and based only on pure experience, free of subjective, inter-pretive elements); thus, philosophy is a totally objective science that endeavors to exclude from knowledge all ideas not included in the realm of experience (the given). Chief works: *Kritik der reinen Erfahrung* (1888-90); *Der Mensch-liche Weltbegriff* (1891).

**Avenpace** (c. 1090-1138). Born as Ibn Badjdja, he was a high dignitary in Islamic Spain until murdered by his enemies, who accused him of atheism and of belittling the validity of the *Koran*. He wrote many commentaries on the works of Aristotle, as well as a famous treatise called *The Hermit's Guide*, which influenced such Scholastic philosophers as THOMAS AQUINAS and ALBERTUS MAGNUS. His own philosophy distinguished between *animal* and *human* activities: human activity is a manifestation of the human intellect; the human intellect is the *emanation* of the Supreme Being; thus, true knowledge consists in a mystical union between man and God.

**Averroës** (1126-1198). Born at Cordova, Spain, as Mohammed ibn Roshd, he taught that there is one eternal truth which can be formulated and comprehended in two ways: through revelation (The Koran); and through natural knowledge (philosophy). He maintained also the doctrine of the *double truth* (a proposition may be theologically true and philosophically false, and vice versa). Although an important Islamic philosopher in his own right, he is renowned mainly for his detailed commentaries on ARISTOTLE. He had a great influence on Catholic philosophers in the Middle Ages, causing *Averroism* to be condemned by the Church. He was also condemned by Mohammedan clergy, and his doctrines and books were banned. Key work: *On the Unification of Philosophy and Religion* (c. 1160).

**Avicebron** (1021-1070). Also known as Solomon ibn Gabirol, he was born at Malaga, Spain. He was the first important Jewish philosopher in Spain. His main work, *Fons Vitae (Fountain of Life)*, became influential and was often referred to by Scholastic thinkers. Basically Platonic in his philosophy, his doctrine of a spiritual substance that individualizes pure spirits or separate forms was opposed by AQUINAS, but found favor with medieval followers of Au-

GUSTINE. He also taught the necessity of a mediator between God and the created world, that mediator being the divine will emanating from God and functioning as a kind of engine of the world.

**Avicenna** (980-1037). Born at Bokhara, Persia, as Ibn Sina, he died at Hamadan. His fame as a physician survived his influence as a philosopher, at least in the West. But he is still held in high esteem as an Islamic philosopher. His philosophy was highly influenced by ARISTOTLE. He embraced Aristotle's *dualism,* but put it differently: *cause* and *effect* are simultaneous, rather than the latter flowing from the former; therefore, God and the world are co-eternal. Chief work: an eighteen volume encyclopedia divided into four subjects: (logic, physics, mathematics, metaphysics); *The Soul,* a poem (c. 1030).

**Axelrod, Djubov Isaac** (1896-1946). Born in Russia, he studied philosophy in Switzerland and became a leading defender of the *materialism* of MARX. Using the dialectic of HEGEL, he tried to expound Marxism as a metaphysical system. He viewed knowledge as the functional, dynamic rapport between the *subject* (the experiencing *knower*) and the *object* (the *known* in experience); in other words, experience is the core of knowledge, and the *experiential act* of knowing is identical to the *experiential existence* of the thing known. The method of knowing is, therefore, a dialectic; however, the dialectic is not only a method, it is also the process which, since knowledge is contained *in* it, is identical to reality itself. From this he concluded that what he called the *dialectical materialism* of Marx, because it satisfied the rules of knowledge and focused upon true reality, was correct and justified. Key work: *The Dialectical Idealism of Hegel and the Dialectical Materialism of Marx* (1934).

**Ayer, Alfred J.** (1910-  ). English thinker and a professor of philosophy at the Universities of Oxford and London. He is

16

known mainly for his work in *empiricism* and *linguistic analysis.* He rejects metaphysics and confines the function of philosophy to analysis. Key works: *Language, Truth and Logic* (1936); *The Foundations of Empirical Knowledge* (1940).

# B

**Baader, Franz Xavier von** (1765-1841). Born at Munich, he was a significant German Catholic thinker who developed the philosophy of *conscience*. He claimed that human knowledge is derived directly from the greater knowledge of God; that man's perception of God's knowledge is, however, only fragmentary and limited; finally, that God gave man the faculty of conscience so that man, in however limited a way, can share in the infinite knowledge of God. *Conscience,* then, according to Baader, should be the criterion of knowledge — everything that satisfies the conscience is correct. Key works: *On Philosophical Dynamism* (1809); *Dogmatic Speculations* (1827-38).

**Bachelard, Gaston** (1884-1962). Born at Bar-sur-Aube, France. A postman in his youth, he prepared to be a scientist and became (1919) a college professor of science. He then turned to philosophy, teaching first at the Univ. of Dijon, then at the Sorbonne. As a young thinker he devoted his attention to the problems raised by the nature of scientific knowledge, especially physics.

From the philosophy of science he turned to a revolutionary investigation of aesthetics, out of which came his philosophy of *imagination*. He distinguished between two forms of imagination: the *formal* and the *material,* and found them both at work in nature, as well as in the mind. *Formal imagination* is the cause of all the unnecessary or picturesque things in nature and the mind, whereas *material imagination* is the cause of eternal and permanent things. Thus, he saw material imagination at work in all things. He analyzed the poetry deriving from this imagination, concluding that reality consists basically of a poetry of imagination. Key works: *Psychoanalysis of Fire* (1938); *The Poetics of Space* (1960).

**Bacon, Francis** (1561-1626). Born in London, and educated in legal and political affairs, he eventually became Lord Chancellor of Great Britain. He was subsequently accused and convicted of accepting bribes from litigants (1621); he retired from public life and spent his remaining years in scientific research. He was the author of the first philosophical work to be written in English: *The Advancement of Learning* (1605). Scientifically oriented and against the prevalent Scholastic methods of logic derived from ARISTOTLE, he proposed a new system for discovering truth: *inductive logic*, known as the *Baconian method* (a fourfold process — empirical observation, analysis of observed data, inference resulting in hypotheses, and verification of hypotheses through further observation and experiment). Main works: *The Advancement of Learning* (1605); *Novum Organum* (1620).

**Bacon, Roger** (1214-1292). A Franciscan monk educated at Oxford and the Univ. of Paris. Primarily a mathematician, he recognized the significance of the deductive application of principles, but only on the condition that the results would be verified through experiment and observation. Chief works: *Opus Majus,* a veritable encyclopedia of the sciences of his day; *Astronomical Speculations* (1277-78).

**Baconthorpe, John** (c. 1300-1346). An English thinker, he was born at Norfolk and was known as the "Resolute Doctor". He was one of the chief interpreters of the philosophy of

AVERROËS and subscribed to the view that truth can be equally discovered through religion or philosophy. His many writings were extremely popular during the Middle Ages.

**Bagehot, Walter** (1826-1877). English historical philosopher who advocated the *cyclical theory of history* (i.e. history progresses in an upward spiral) as earlier advanced by VICO. He held that there have been *three* outstanding periods in the spiral of history: (1) the custom-making epoch; (2) the age of conflict; (3) the era of discussion. Each has elevated the human spirit to a level higher than the preceding. He concluded that the spiral movement would necessarily continue to carry man even higher.

**Bakunin, Michael** (1814-1876). Born near Moscow, this Russian socialist thinker was important for his opposition to MARX. He advocated a form of worldwide social democracy based on *anarchism*. Not a violent anarchism, however. Anarchism, as he envisioned it, was the very opposite of violence. It was law-less, therefore not lawless. In other words, he felt that man is corrupted by laws and that by the abolition of all laws, the causes of rebellion would be removed. Key work: *The Revolutionary Catechism* (1871).

**Baldwin, James Mark** (1861-1934). American psychologist born at Columbia, South Carolina, he also wrote extensively in philosophy. His main contribution lay in his advancement of a new kind of logic — the *logic of relativity*. He felt that truth lies in the correlation of different, and at times antagonistic, opinions. Truth flows through all things, but human understanding of it is — like a snapshot — only a partial, isolated picture of the total panorama. The *logic of relativity*, then, was designed to foster a type of thinking that would give the mind a cinematic, rather than a snapshot, quality, so that the mind could study reality as a flowing stream or an unfolding world, and correlate all its

21

images into a cohesive, unified and whole truth. Key works: *Social and Ethical Interpretations in Mental Development* (1894); *The Story of the Mind* (1898).

**Barth, Karl** (1886-   ). Swiss Christian philosopher and theologian. He holds that God is wholly *other than* man and totally beyond man's rational apprehension; the only way to attain God is through explicit faith in his existence and trust in his divine plan for salvation as expressed through Revelation. His system is known as *dialectical theology* because of its emphasis upon the contradiction between God and the world. This position is summarized in one of his chief works: *The Knowledge of God and the Science of God* (1939).

**Batteux, Charles** (1713-1780). French religious philosopher born at Alland'huy, he was educated at the Univ. of Rheims and later taught philosophy at the College of France. His primary philosophical concern was with *aesthetics* — he held that man is born with an intrinsic sense of beauty which permits him to understand the beautiful in nature; hence, art is not just a copy of life, but man's endeavor to define the beautiful. Since the sense of beauty is God-given, art is the ultimate endeavor to define God. Key work: *The Beautiful Arts* (1746).

**Baumgarten, Alexander Gottlieb** (1714-1762). German thinker of the period prior to KANT. He introduced the term *aesthetics* (the philosophy of beauty) and held that beauty is the recognition of perfection by means of the senses. Chief work: *Aesthetica.*

**Bax, Ernest Belfort** (1854-1926). Born at Leamington, England, he was a student of the philosophies of KANT and HEGEL, and later advanced his own doctrine that the best way to promote a practical, working ethics is through politics. As a result, he devoted most of his energy to advancing a theory

22

of social democracy in which the concept of *justice* was paramount. Key works: *Essays in Socialism* (1906); *Problems of Men, Mind and Morals* (1912).

**Bayle, Pierre** (1647-1706). French philosopher of history who spent much of his adult life in exile in Rotterdam, Holland, because of his opposition to the oppressive reign of Louis XIV in France. He was an advocate of objectivity in every respect, and what interested him in history was not only historical facts, but the use and interpretation men make of such facts. His *Historical and Critical Dictionary* was an attempt to render historical facts with pure objectivity and to show that the conventional methods of history were too interpretative and colored by the prejudices of those who compiled it. He refuted the "double theory" of philosophy which held that reason could not function without revelation; he claimed that faith is irrelevant in any attempt to understand the world and that facts are what count.

**Beattie, James** (1735-1803). Scottish thinker who attacked HUME for advocating an *atheistic nihilism* in his doctrine that nothing really exists, but that everything is a figment of the mind. Beattie maintained that the world does indeed have a morality outside of the mind that perceives it. Key work: *Essay on Truth* (1770).

**Beneke, Friedrich Eduard** (1798-1854). A German thinker who followed the *idealism* of KANT but modified it with *empiricism* (i.e. knowledge is attainable only through experience and observation). He exerted much influence on psychological and educational theories of the 19th century. Key works: *New Foundations of Metaphysics* (1822); *Metaphysics and Philosophy of Religion* (1840).

**Bentham, Jeremy** (1748-1832). Born in London, he was the founder of English *utilitarian* philosophy. Remembered as a legal and political critic and reformer, he was also the most influential social philosopher of his time. He introduced the *greatest happiness* principle to ethics (i.e. happiness is identical with pleasure; we all desire happiness, this being the underlying motive of human behavior; therefore, providing the greatest and continuing pleasure should be the aim of government, so that peace and harmony will prevail in society). Chief works: *Principles of Morals and Legislation* (1789).

**Berdyaev, Nikolai Alexandrovitch** (1874-1948). Contemporary Russian philosopher of religion. Born at Kiev, he was at first a Marxist but was arrested (1898) for his socialist activities and banished to the north of Russia (Vologda) for three years. He reverted to Christianity (1905) but was accused of insulting the Synod of the Orthodox Church (1914). His trial (1917) was terminated by the Russian Revolution. He was then expelled from the Soviet Union by the communist government because of his outspoken support of Christianity. His remaining years were spent first in Berlin, where he opened a school, then in Paris.

His philosophy conceives of man as the conjunction of the natural and divine worlds. Man, created by the creator, must necessarily continue the creative process in order to prove the creative character of his cognitive faculty, using this for the perfection of true civilization. His thought resembles that of the early Christian Gnostics (who sought to transcend rational thought processes by intuition in order to arrive at truth) and is often called a form of *Christian existentialism*. Chief works: *The Meaning of History* (1923); *Freedom and the Spirit* (1935).

**Bergson, Henri** (1859-1941). Born in Paris, France, of a Jewish family, he was a professor of philosophy at various schools in France and won the Nobel Prize (1927). His philosophy was aimed at upsetting the dogmatic naturalism and the mechanistic, static materialism which reached their heights in the late 19th century and to which he had originally

24

subscribed. The vital center of his metaphysics is his idea of *duration,* as opposed to the mechanistic concept of *time.* *Duration* is the original *thing-in-itself,* that which philosophy has always called *substance;* except that to Bergson it is a specific experience, revealed to the individual in his immediate experience. Thus, all things (matter, time, motion, the absolute, etc.) are but so many specialized forms of duration. His phrase *elan vital* sums up his *vitalistic* doctrine that there is an original life force, and that it passes from one generation of living beings to another by way of developed individual organisms. From this stems his belief in the unlimited progress of humanity. He also dealt considerably with *intuition,* describing it as the dynamic key to rational knowledge. Chief works: *Matter and Memory* (1896); *Two Sources of Morality and Religion* (1932).

**Berkeley, George** (1685-1753). He was born at Kilkenny, Ireland, and died at Oxford, England. Later in life, he was appointed Bishop of Cloyne, Ireland (Anglican Church). He was a champion of *religious idealism.* His philosophy was directed to proving God's existence and His role as the true cause of all things. He employed LOCKE's philosophy concerning human knowledge, stressing the distinction between ideas and the mind itself. He conceived of the mind as an active being, separate from its content, and concluded that reality consists of and exists only in the mind; that is, nothing exists except minds (spirits) and their contents (ideas). Similarly, God is the universal Mind and the ideas contained in this Mind constitute the natural world. Reality, then, is composed of spirits and ideas, while the physical aspects of the world are nothing but mental phenomena. Major work: *Treatise on the Principles of Human Knowledge* (1710).

**Bernard of Chartres** (died c. 1130). Little is known about him except that he taught in the school of Chartres, France (1114-

25

1119) and was Chancellor of Chartres (1119-1124). Extremely Platonistic, he was a *realist* in his theory of *universals,* but taught that the forms of things *(formae nativae)* are distinct from the exemplary ideas in the divine mind. A treatise, *De Expositione Porphyrii,* has been attributed to him.

**Bhartri-Hari** (c. 600-660). Hindu philosopher who subscribed to the doctrine of *renunciation* (i.e. to be free from fear, man must be free from desire; hence, man should renounce the objects and materials that provoke desire).

**Blanshard, Brand** (1892-    ). Born at Sutton, Massachusetts, he teaches at Yale University and has become a significant American thinker. In philosophy, he has ascribed the development of thought to psychological and rationalistic causes. He is basically a *rational idealist* (i.e. everything in reality is the "idea" of a Universal Mind, and man's reason is the link to that Mind). He further claims that all human thoughts are interconnected through Universal Mind. Key work: *The Nature of Thought* (1939).

**Blondel, Maurice** (1861-1949). French philosopher who was born at Dijon and died at Aix-en-Provence. He propounded a philosophy of *action* (which seeks a compromise in the relation between thought and action and between the extremes of intellectualism and pragmatism in order to find a proper mean by which to guide all endeavor). He later gave his activistic philosophy a strong theological emphasis. Chief works: *Action* (1893); *The Process of Intelligence* (1922); *Being and Beings* (1935).

**Boehme, Jakob** (1575-1624). Born at Gorlitz, Germany, he received little formal schooling. He became noted as a mystic and theosophist, and had many followers in Germany and Russia. He regarded the universe as a theatre in which the eternal conflict between matter and spirit is played out; matter is evil, but as necessary to existence as spirit, which is good. All reality, then, according to him, contains a duality of good and evil — even God. Key work: *The Two Principles of Divine Essence* (1615).

**Boethius** (480-525). An influential commentator on ARISTOTLE who, in his own thought, reflected neo-Platonic influences. As a minister to the Byzantine emperor Theodoric, he was accused of being a traitor and sentenced to death. It was while he awaited execution that he wrote his universally known work, *On the Consolation of Philosophy,* a testament to faith in man and belief in the Divine Will.

His philosophy demands love of wisdom, love of God, and human participation in beatitude and divine perfection. He described God as existing in an *eternal present,* and said that God does not "pre-see" but that He "fore-sees."

**Bolzano, Bernard** (1781-1848). Czech philosopher and mathematician, and professor of philosophy at the Univ. of Prague (1805-1820). He was compelled to resign because of his rationalistic tendencies in theology, and held no further academic positions. His chief work, *Wissenschaftslehre* (1837), while a study of traditional logic, contains significant anticipations of many ideas that have since become vital to symbolic logic and mathematics, especially the theory of transfinite numbers. Other key works: *Reasons for the Immortality of the Soul* (1826); *Paradoxes of Infinity* (1836).

**Bonaventure** (1221-1274). A contemporary and colleague of THOMAS AQUINAS, he was born at Bagnorea, Italy, under the name of Giovanni di Fidenza. He joined the Franciscans (1238), received a licentiate in theology from Univ. of Paris (1248), and taught at Paris for seven years thereafter. He was then elected Superior-General of the Franciscan order (1257) and subsequently became a cardinal of the

Church (1273). He died while attending the Council of Lyons.

His philosophy was basically Augustinian and theologically directed, with some Aristotelian modifications as reflected in his theory of the *duality of knowledge* (i.e. there are two kinds of knowledge: *human,* from science; and *mystical,* from divine grace). Key work: *Outline of the Mind in God* (1259).

**Boodin, John Elof** (1869-1950). Born in Sweden, he emigrated to the U.S. (1886) and studied at Harvard under ROYCE, with whom he maintained a life-long friendship. His highly systematized philosophy constitutes a form of *cosmic idealism* (i.e. the cosmos is a structure consisting of a hierarchy of *fields,* as exemplified in such things as physics, organisms, consciousness, society, etc.). From this comes a concept of reality made up of five components: *being, time, space, consciousness* and *form.* God is the spirit of the whole. Major works: *Time and Reality* (1904); *Truth and Reality* (1911); *Cosmic Evolution* (1925); *Three Interpretations of the Universe* (1934).

**Boole, George** (1815-1864). English mathematician born at Lincoln, he taught at Queen's College in Ireland (1849-1864). He was the founder of Boolean algebra and the 19th century algebra of logic, the foundations of modern symbolic logic. Major works: *Mathematical Analysis of Logic* (1847); *Laws of Thought* (1854).

**Bosanquet, Bernard** (1848-1923). Next to BRADLEY, he is the best known of the English philosophers of *idealism.* He was born at Rock Hall, England, and died in London. He taught philosophy for 11 years at Oxford, then retired to devote himself to the study of ethics, logic and aesthetics. His philosophy regarded a particular form of reality (i.e. a wholly universal and concrete experience) as that which alone exists; all other particulars (e.g., minds, objects) contain universality and concreteness only partially, therefore they only partially exist. To achieve complete existence requires subjugation of the individual to the cosmic drama, whose author is the Absolute; in this drama the individual undergoes a dramatic *catharsis* (i.e. enlightenment under the pressure of intellectual and emotional conflict) and is thrust toward self-realization and towards the perfection of complete existence. Major works: *Logic* (1888); *The Philosophical Theory of the State* (1899); *Value and Destiny of the Individual* (1913); *A History of Aesthetics* (1921).

**Boscovich, Ruggero Giuseppe** (1711-1787). Born in Dalmatia, he became an important metaphysical thinker in Italy. He taught at various Italian universities, and died at Milan. He developed a complex doctrine of *dynamic, mechanistic nature* not unlike that of LEIBNIZ. He conceived of nature as being made up of *simple substances* (immaterial atoms) in consistent and reciprocal relationships to one another; these atoms represent *pure being* and it is precisely in their relationship that true reality is found. From this *atomic dynamism* all extensions of reality derive, including material things. For instance, matter itself is constituted of a relationship of atoms; in its essence, this relationship is power, and its material manifestations (motion, volume, dimension, etc.) are the tangible effects of that power. The diversity of things is a result not of the ultimate elements themselves (atoms), but, again, the result of the ever-changing but constant relationship between the atoms that constitute *pure being*. Thus it is, then, that all things derive atomically from *pure being*. Key work: *On Space and Time* (1763).

**Boutroux, Emile** (1845-1921). The teacher of BERGSON and BLONDEL, and a French *spiritualist* thinker, he is noted for his defense of the doctrines of *contingency* and *indeterminacy* (as against *necessity* and *determinacy*) in metaphysics. He demonstrated that the concept of natural law in all the sciences is a result rather than a principle, for it does not prove the universal reign of necessity (that which *must* be); this being so, contingency (that which *may be*) becomes the principle of both natural science and metaphysics, and man is able to act upon nature. Main work: *Contingency of the Laws of Nature* (tr. 1920).

**Bowne, Borden Parker** (1847-1910). An American, he was for many years a teacher of philosophy at Boston University. He was born at Leonardville, New Jersey. His philosophy had a theological bias and was conspicuous for its combining of *theism* with *idealism*. He termed and developed the philosophy of *personalism* (i.e. the personality, be it divine or human or other, is the supreme value of and key to understanding reality). Main works: *Theory of Thought and Knowledge* (1897); *Personalism* (1908).

**Brabant.** See SIGER DE BRABANT.

**Bradley, Francis Herbert** (1846-1924). Born at Glasbury, Wales, he was England's leading *idealist* philosopher and spent practically all his life at Oxford, both as student and teacher. He employed Hegelian dialectic but repudiated HEGEL'S form of idealism. Instead, he built his own *absolute idealism* without any scheme of categories. Accordingly, he disrupted modern theories of being and knowledge, especially with his famous doctrine of the *degrees of truth* (truth can only reside in judgment; not all judgments are true; when a subject is careful and sufficiently inclusive, its judgment approaches truth; truth really requires the Absolute). His analysis gradually developed the realization of a universal and coherent unity, infinite in character. Chief works: *Appearance and Reality* (1893); *Essays on Truth and Reality* (1914).

**Braithwaite, Richard Bevan** (1900-   ). English philosopher and a professor of moral philosophy at the Univ. of Cambridge, his principal contribution derives from his complex efforts to make *religious beliefs* acceptable to *empiricism* (i.e. the sole source of knowledge is experience), and in putting moral choice on a rational basis. Toward these ends he has applied the mathematical *theory of games* (a probability theory developed by statisticians for the purpose of making choices between statistical hypotheses). His use of this theory provides a logical procedure of rejection as well as one of choice, and so guarantees that statements of probability can have an empirical meaning. Key work: *Scientific Explanation* (1953).

**Brentano, Franz** (1838-1916). Born at Marienberg, Germany, he became a Roman Catholic priest (1864). He abandoned the priesthood (1873) and became a professor at Wuerzburg and then at Vienna. His thought was based on the assertion that psychology was the only basis for philosophy and the proper path to metaphysics. He did not believe in metaphysical systems but felt that truth is attainable through two forms of psychic activity (representation and judgment), and that all psychological phenomena refer to an object. Both of these views were the basis of his doctrine of *intentionalism*. Key works: *The Origin of Moral Knowledge* (1889); *The Psychology of Sensations* (1907); *Psychology From the Empirical Point of View* (1924-29).

**Bridgman, Percy W.** (1882-1961). Born at Cambridge, Massachusetts, he was for many years a professor of mathematics and philosophy at Harvard, noted for his *operational theory of meaning*. Dissatisfied with the inadequacy of classical physical concepts, he redefined *concept* as a set of operations comprised of mental and physical activity, and claimed that truth is identical with verifiability (that which is verifiable is true) and that the criterion, therefore, of truth is the scientific method (experiment and observation). He then broadened this view into social philosophy, declaring that man's most satisfactory pursuit is the attempt to conquer his innate lack of rationality through operational conceptual activity (i.e. apprehending the relations, consequences and implications of his drive for intelligent, orderly life). Chief works: *The Nature of Physical Theory* (1936); *The Intelligent Individual and Society* (1938).

**Broad, Charlie Dunbar** (1887-    ). Contemporary English critical philosopher born in London, he formulated a highly sophisticated system based on a theory of *emergent materialism* (i.e. everything happens by the blind combination of the elements of matter or energy, without any guidance). Chief works: *The Mind and its Place in Nature* (1925); *Five Types of Ethical Theory* (1930).

**Brochard, Victor** (1848-1907). French thinker born at Quesnoy-sur-Deûle. He is most noted for his work entitled *On Error* (1879), in which he attempted to show the lack of distinction between the true and the false, taken in themselves and independent of any activity of verification. "Truth is something that a hypothesis can not confirm," he wrote, "and falsity is something that a hypothesis can not refute."

**Bruno, Giordano** (1548-1600). An Italian by birth and a Dominican monk by vocation, he was eventually burned at the stake during the Italian Inquisition because of his refusal to recant views which were considered highly heretical.

He subscribed to a naturalistic and mystic *pantheism* (i.e. God is nature) conditioned by Copernican astronomy. For him, God and the universe were two names for one and the same reality. This reality he conceived of as existing in a kind of co-equal duality; *natura naturans,* the wholeness, transcendence and unity of nature; and *natura naturata,* the infinity of worlds, objects and events of which the whole is composed. The world-process, then, is a perpetual out-flow and return of the divine nature from and to itself; the human mind represents the apogee of the outflow and marks also, in the exercise of its rational powers, the point at which the reverse movement of the divine nature returning-to-itself begins. The human soul, participating in this ebb and flow of the divine nature, returns at the body's death to God, whence it came, to be re-absorbed in Him. Main philosophical work: *On the Infinite, the Universe, and the World* (1584).

**Brunschwicg, Leon** (1869-1944). Born in Paris, he was a professor of philosophy at the Ecole Normale in Paris. His thought is an *idealistic* synthesis of that of SPINOZA, KANT and SCHELLING, with special stress placed on the creative role of thought in the history of culture. Main works: *Human Experience and Physical Causality* (1921); *Knowledge of the Self* (1931).

**Buber, Martin** (1878-1965). Born in Vienna, he has become the leading philosopher of Judaism in this century. He taught at the Univ. of Frankfurt (1923-33) before being expelled from Germany by the Nazi regime. He emigrated to Palestine, where he settled and continued to teach. His work, although basically theological in nature, is concerned with man's relation to the universe — he terms man's quest for truth and God an "experience of unity." Key work: *I and Thou* (1923).

**Büchner, Ludwig** (1824-1899). German philosopher who, through his book *Power and Matter,* made materialism a popular doctrine in Central Europe. He opposed dualism, claiming that the soul is merely a function of the brain.

**Buckle, Henry Thomas** (1821-1862). English philosopher of history, born in Kent. He held that history demonstrates the influence of *geography* on human character. Not only do the location and climate of a country determine the nature and habits of its inhabitants, but the inhabitants instinctively seek to improve their nature by changing their environment. Key work: *History of Civilization* (1860-62).

**Buddha, Gautama** (c. 563-483 B. C.). Born Siddhartha Gautama, a prince, at Kapilavastu in what is now northern India, he gave up the life of royalty in early manhood and plunged himself into anonymous poverty in order to seek wisdom and truth. He spent many years in solitary meditation, during which he arrived at the view that the cause of human misery and sorrow was the endless succession of births and deaths in the turbulent stream of existence. He saw existence as a tedious round of birth, life, desire, frustration and death — repeated over and over again. Since all humans were reborn again, death was merely a transition from life to life and the process of existence was endless. This, he concluded, was the source of human despair.

With this view in mind, he set out to show how despair could be alleviated. He offered two alternatives. The first was to put a direct end to the continual succession of re-births. But this was impossible — the law of the Karma would not permit it. The whole point of this law was to provide retribution for the sins of our present life through our re-birth into another life. Since the law would not permit the first alternative, the only other choice was to remove the cause for retribution. If sin and evil could be toppled, there would no longer be a need for the law of retribution and the cycle of despair would come to a halt. By living a life of perfect justice and virtue, man could eliminate sin and evil. The state of life required to achieve this ideal condition he called *Nirvana* — the core of Buddha's subsequent philosophy.

*Nirvana* is the ultimate liberation of the soul — man's rejection of the bondage of his earthly desires so that his soul can enter unhindered into a state of unity between itself and the universe. Again, the ultimate purpose of achieving *Nirvana* is the extinction of sin, for by ridding himself of sin man rids himself of the causes of retribution and rebirth, and thereby despair. Buddha propounded a doctrine of love as the best means of achieving *Nirvana* and spent the rest of his life in the practice of this doctrine. Today, Buddhism is the religion of over half a billion people — about one-sixth of the world's population.

**Buridan, Jean** (c. 1300-1365). Born at Bethune, France, he studied under WILLIAM OF OCKHAM but later (1340), as Rector of the Univ. of Paris, repudiated his teacher's thought for its *nominalism*. He himself was a *determinist* who believed that the will as such had no freedom to make decisions and is in fact controlled entirely by the intellect. He also studied physics and concluded, in opposition to ARISTOTLE, that all movement is the result of *impetus* and is not caused. Key work: *Philosophy of Nature*.

**Burke, Edmund** (1729-1797). Irish political philosopher, he was born in Dublin and died in London. His philosophy was primarily based on a doctrine of *conciliation* (i.e. in all political controversies, especially between the old and the new, the *middle course* is the wisest approach to resolving them). Key works: *On the Origin of Our Ideas of the Sublime and Beautiful* (1757); *Reflections on the French Revolution* (1790).

# C

**Caird, Edward** (1835-1908). Scottish philosopher who was educated and held teaching positions at the Univ. of Glasgow. His main concern was to reconcile theology to philosophy in order to show that revelation and reason seek to ascertain the same thing — that the *good* is identical with God. Key works: *The Critical Philosophy of Immanuel Kant* (1889); *Essays on Literature and Philosophy* (1893).

**Calkins, Mary Whiton** (1863-1930). American thinker who was born at Hartford, Connecticut and who spent 39 years as a professor of philosophy at Wellesley College. She also made contributions to psychology. Considerably influenced by the philosophy of ROYCE, she termed her idealistic thought *absolutistic personalism*. She proceeded from the conviction that the universe contains distinct mental realities; that although the mind originally emerged from a lower level of existence, it no longer belongs to that level but rather to a new order of existence which has special laws of behavior. These mental realities are ultimately personal, since consciousness never occurs impersonally. She also asserted that the universe is, throughout, mental, and that whatever is real is ultimately mental and therefore personal. Chief works: *The Persistent Problems of Philosophy* (1907); *The Good Man and The Good* (1918).

**Callicles** (c. 415-350 B. C.). Ancient Greek philosopher who advanced the theory — later adapted by Nietzsche — that the only justice in the world is the *selfishness* of the strong as opposed to the *selflessness* of the weak; in other words, greater powers should subdue lesser powers. He postulated this as a law of nature and insisted that if man were to subscribe to it, peace and harmony would reign.

**Campanella, Tomasso** (1568-1639). A Dominican monk who was born in Naples, he was sentenced to lifetime imprisonment for heresy. During this time he wrote a defense and vindication of Galileo, who had been condemned by the Roman Inquisition. After 27 years in prison, he escaped to France where he remained the rest of his life under the aegis of Cardinal Richelieu.

Philosophically, he repudiated Aristotelianism, embraced *naturalism,* and anticipated some of the conclusions of DES- CARTES. He belittled both sense knowledge and rational knowledge and based his views on the assertion that the facts of one's own existence are the only criteria of truth, as well as inferences therefrom (thus, if I exist, then all things I see and conceive must exist). He is remembered most as a political philosopher who conceived of a utopia built along Platonic lines but infused with religious control and ruled by an ideal Pope. Main work: *City of the Sun.*

**Cantoni, Carlo** (1840-1906). Italian philosopher who rejected Kant's doctrine of the *subjective-objective* (*noumena-phenomena*) nature of man's relation to the world, and who proposed a doctrine of *monism* in its stead (i.e. the world consists of a single entity of substance-and-mind blended in an indivisible unity; hence, man's knowledge of the world is *immediate* through intuitive consciousness). Key works: *Elementary Course in Philosophy* (1870-71); *Kant* (1879-84).

**Cantor, Georg** (1845-1918). Russian-born German mathematician and a professor of mathematics at Halle (1872-1913). He is important to philosophy for his contributions to the foundations to mathematical analysis and as the founder of the theory of *transfinite cardinal and ordinal numbers.*

**Carlyle, Thomas** (1795-1881). Vigorous and outspoken Scottish historian and essayist who propounded a political philosophy based on a doctrine of *work.* He was born at Ecclefecham, Scotland, and died in London. An admirer of German idealism, and of German culture in general, he distrusted the principles of democracy and espoused a patriarchal mode of government that was a compound of Christian principles and quasi-Fascist methods. Major works: *Heroes and Hero Worship* (1840); *The French Revolution* (1837).

**Carnap, Rudolph** (1891-  ). Born in Germany, he was a professor of philosophy successively at the Universities of Vienna, Prague and Chicago. He was a founder of what is known as the Vienna Circle and became one of the leading representatives of *scientific empiricism.*

His thought was devoted almost exclusively to formal logic and its applications to problems of epistemology (the theory of knowledge) and science. He felt that the task of philosophy is the analysis of knowledge, especially of science; and that the proper method for this is the analysis of the language of science. He helped to develop a new science of *logical syntax* and *semantics* (the analysis of language to test the validity of propositions). He also espoused the doctrine of *physicalism* (every descriptive term used in the language of sciences is connected with terms designating observable properties of things) and sought to construct one common unified language for all branches of empirical science so that problems of language would no longer be an impediment to knowledge. Key works: *The Logical Syntax of Language* (1934); *Introduction to Semantics* (1942); *The Logical Foundations of Probability* (1950).

**Carneades** (c. 215-129 B. C.). An opponent of the *Stoic* school of Greek philosophy and a director of the Platonic Academy in Athens, his most noteworthy contribution to thought consisted in the fact that he was one of the earliest to develop the doctrine of *logical probabilism,* which holds that certainty is unattainable and that probability is the only guide to belief and action. He claimed that the truth of an idea can only be probable, not certain; one discovers probable truth by means of critical analysis, synthesis and comparison.

**Carriere, Moritz** (1817-1895). German thinker born at Griedel, he is significant for his efforts to reconcile *deism* (i.e. a belief in God, but a non-parochial, non-personal God) and *pantheism* (i.e. a belief that the combination of everything in the universe constitutes God).

**Carus, Paul** (1852-1919). American religious philosopher, he was born at Isenburg, Germany, and died at Chicago. He was, to a degree, an advocate of the doctrine of *monism* (i.e. matter is identical with mind, and there is no duality of mind and matter). He explained God as man's symbol for the cosmic harmony of the universe.

**Cassirer, Ernst** (1874-1945). Scientific philosopher born at Breslau, Germany, he was compelled to emigrate from Germany by the Hitler regime. He taught for a short time at Goetenborg, Sweden; he then entered the U. S. and subsequently became a professor of philosophy at Columbia Univ.

Very much influenced by the thought of HERMANN COHEN, he is noted for his philosophy of history, which proceeds from the conviction that historical investigation and systematic order are not contradictory but are mutually supportive. Thus, there is an *immanent logic of history.* His principal significance to philosophy was in his consideration of the functions of linguistic and mystical thinking, in which he coordinated the world of pure knowledge with religious,

40

mystical and artistic ideas. He concluded that the different approaches to reality cooperate in the formation of a totality of meaning. Main works: *Substance and Function* (1910); *Philosophy of Symbolic Form* (1923).

**Cebes** (c. 475-425 B.C.). A Greek thinker who was a friend and disciple of SOCRATES. The heart of his philosophy centered in his declaration that true happiness can come only from true knowledge. He appears as one of the characters in Plato's *Phaedo*, where he argues against the immortality of the soul. Main work: *Pinax* (a dialogue that became very popular during the Middle Ages).

**Celsus** (c. 112-164). A Greek philosopher and a strong proponent of the *idealism* of PLATO, he is most noteworthy as one of the earliest critics of Christianity. His book *A True Discourse* maligned the Christians mainly because their philosophy was derived from that of the Jews.

**Chang Hêng-ch'ü** (1020-1076). Born in Chensi, China, he studied thoroughly the doctrines of Taoism and Buddhism before becoming an advocate of Confucianism. A *materialist,* he claimed that the world is ruled by the perpetual contraction and expansion of a mass of air, which he called *primordial breath.*

**Ch'êng I-Chüan** (1033-1107). The younger brother of CH'ÊNG MING-TAO, he was born at Hopei, China. He was probably the first *rationalist* thinker of Confucian philosophy. He distinguished between the *spiritual plan* and the *material plan* of the world, and concluded that matter and spirit are co-equal and co-necessary to existence. As for man, the spiritual part of his nature is pure; it is his exposure to material things that corrupts his nature. Also, his acts are conditioned by the extent of his knowledge; thus, the superior man seeks at all times to develop his knowledge.

41

**Ch'êng Ming-tao** (1032-1086). A foremost Chinese thinker who, with his brother, CH'ÊNG I-CH'UAN repudiated Taoism and Buddhism and instead developed new aspects of Confucianism. Born at Hopei, he still ranks as one of the great neo-Confucians in Chinese philosophy.

He was principally an *idealist;* he believed that the universe came from a *mixture* of primordial substances. He explained the different character and quality of things by his view that all things receive the *mixture* in different ways. Man receives the most *mixture,* thus is the highest of things. In ethics, his views were relative — for instance, *evil* has no reality in itself, it is merely an excess of *good.*

**Chestov, Leon** (1866-1938). Born at Kiev, Russia, he emigrated to France and died in Paris. Strongly influenced by NIETZSCHE and Dostoievsky, he developed a *philosophy of tragedy,* through which he proclaimed the absurdity of human existence. He felt that man's central problem was the fact that he possesses reason — that reason works in such a way as to transform reality into necessity, thus destroying man's freedom. This deprivation of freedom creates in man a *nostalgia* for it. It was this nostalgia that Chestov sought to awaken and to transform into *active will,* for only by the activation of the will can man overcome the bondage of his conscience.

**Chernyshevsky, Nikolai** (1828-1889). Born at Saratov, Russia, he was a rigorous political thinker and an outspoken critic of Tsarist government. He was exiled to Siberia (1862). However, his writings still had great attraction for the oppressed of Russia. Because he was deeply captivated by the political and economic doctrines of MILL, his work served to introduce the liberalizing spirit of Western civilization into Russia.

**Chrysippus** (c. 281-205 B. C.). Born at Soli, in Asia Minor, he went to Athens (260 B. C.) and eventually succeeded CLEANTHES as leader of the *Stoic* school of Greek philosophy. He is said to have written some 700 books, all of which are lost. He stated that the essential characteristic of man which distinguishes him from animals is that his judgment becomes active as soon as his sensations are irritated.

**Chuang Chou** (c. 340-280 B. C.). Modern experts on Chinese philosophy consider him among the most brilliant and original of all Chinese thinkers. Versed in dialectic and logic, he advanced a theory of the unity of the universe and longed for the transcendental bliss that would bring peace of mind and enable man to live harmoniously with nature. As a formidable adversary of Confucianism and a developer of Taoism, he was frequently and severely criticized by MEN-CIUS.

**Chu Hsi** (1130-1200). Chinese neo-Confucian thinker who championed the investigation of things and the extension of contemporary knowledge. Born at Nganhouei, he set the model for Confucian orthodoxy until the 20th century. He was basically a *rationalist* who distinguished between a *spiritual* and a *material* principle in the world; however, these dual principles do not act separately — they are always together, and in their interaction are responsible for the eternal cycle of creation and destruction. Chief work: *The Philosophy of Human Nature.*

**Cicero, Marcus Tullius** (106-43 B. C.). Roman political philosopher and historian whose writings had considerable influence on the formation of subsequent societies. He is most noted for his eclectic exposition of general scientific knowledge and philosophy, by which he aimed to arouse an appreciation of Greek culture in the minds of Romans. Key works: *On the Republic* (54-51 B. C.); *Stoic Paradoxes* (46 B. C.).

**Clarke, Samuel** (1675-1729). English religious philosopher, he was born at Norwich and gained fame for his vigorous repudiation of the Catholic dogma of the Trinity. He held that the fundamental principles of morality derive from the *harmony or disharmony of relationships* in the world, and that these principles can be affirmed as scientifically as the truths of mathematics. God controls these relationships; because they are affirmable by reason, God, too, can be affirmed by reason. Key work: *Demonstration of the Being and Attributes of God* (1720).

**Cleanthes** (c. 310-230 B. C.). A disciple of ZENO and one of the early leaders of the *Stoic* school of Greek philosophy, he developed the doctrine of *seminal reason* (i.e. the universal principle of the organization of living beings which is contained, like a self-perpetuating germ, in the law of the universe). But his work was devoted above all to ethics: he claimed that virtue is universal and one — a voluntary assent to the reason that governs nature — and is a kind of tension that animates the world.

**Clement of Alexandria** (150-217). Early Christian thinker and theologian who attempted to raise religious faith to the level of knowledge. Born a pagan, he converted to Christianity at an early age and settled at Alexandria, Egypt. He claimed that reason is as divine a light in the world as revelation; that there is one New Testament, but *two* Old Testaments — the Law of the Hebrews and the philosophy of the Greeks.

**Clitomachus** (c. 180-110 B. C.). Born at Carthage, he was a disciple of Carneades and insisted that philosophy is based on *probabilities* rather than on certainties. Some things seem closer to truth than others; therefore, man should adjust his ethical conduct to fit those propositions that appear to be the most proximate to truth. This point of view was an early forerunner of *pragmatism*.

**Cohen, Hermann** (1842-1918). Born at Coswig, Germany, he became a leader of the Marburg School, which championed the *a priori* method of KANT (i.e. the ability to know by reason alone) and refuted empiricism. He contended that all things knowable are knowable *a priori,* and that reality is nothing else but that which is posited by thought. His philosophy was a reaction against those philosophies that claimed the object of knowledge to be experience. He regarded thought (reason) as "pure creation" — not the result of experience but the condition of it. Along with this, he insisted that all ideas (including the idea of God) have no existence in themselves but are laws or methods of thought, and the principles of life. Thus, only through reason can existence be given to ideas; at the same time, only through ideas can the world be understood, since the world is the product of ideas. Key works: *System of Philosophy; Logic of Pure Knowledge.*

**Cohen, Morris Raphael** (1880-1947). Born at Minsk, Russia, he emigrated to the U. S. (1892) and later enjoyed a long and distinguished career as a professor of philosophy at City College in New York. He held to a view that he called *realistic rationalism,* which emphasized the importance of intellect or reason as applied to *what is,* rather than *in themselves.* He also developed the *principle of polarity* (i.e. opposites involve each other and are not just contradictory) to resolve apparent contradictions in thought. Main work: *Reason and Nature* (1931); *An Introduction to Logic* (with ERNEST NAGEL, 1934).

**Collins, Anthony** (1676-1729). Born at Heston, England, he was an advocate of the philosophy of LOCKE and developed the doctrine of *necessity* (i.e. whatever *is,* is the necessary result of whatever *was*). Because *necessity* is the principle of nature, there can be no such thing as free will. Key work: *On the Use of Reason* (1707).

**Collingwood, Robin George** (1889-1943). An English thinker, he was born at Lancadine and spent his entire adult life as a professor of metaphysics at Oxford Univ. The most distinctive theme of his work is that which identifies philosophy with history. He viewed history as the history of human thought and felt that the task of the historian is to relive, or re-create, the *thoughts* of the figure he treats. Thus, the true historian must be a philosopher, and the ultimate function of philosophy is an historical one — to bring to light the absolute presuppositions of human thought at any given date in history. Key works: *Essay on Philosophical Method* (1933); *Essay on Metaphysics* (1940).

**Comte, Auguste** (1798-1857). Born at Montpelier, France, when social and political conditions were highly unstable, he rose against the tendency prevalent among his predecessors to propound philosophical doctrines that contravened the facts of nature and society. He thus developed what he called *positivism,* which was intended once and for all to put an end to the inherent negativism of endless speculation and assumption and to the controversies deriving therefrom. He died in Paris. To him, philosophy was in the process of being absorbed by science, and he set out to define philosophy historically in three stages: (1) *theology,* where man's speculations were dominated by superstitions and prejudices; (2) *metaphysics,* where man's search for reality took the form of rational speculation unsupportable by facts; (3) *positivism,* where dogmatic assumptions began to be replaced by factual and scientific knowledge. Main work: *The Course of Positive Philosophy* (1830-42).

**Condillac, Etienne** (1715-1780). Born at Grenoble, he was a French *sensationalist* (i.e. all knowledge is derived from the sensations we experience) who, similarly to LOCKE, worked out a system in which all the human faculties are reduced in essence to a sensory basis. Thus, comprehension, in all its phases, is nothing more than the comparison, or multiplication, of the senses. He extended this psychological view to a description of man as being composed of two egos; that of *habit* and that of *reflection.* Habit acts unconsciously, is capable only of the basic senses, and is the source of reason. Chief works: *Essay on the Origin of Human Knowledge* (1746); *Treatise on the Sensations* (1754); *Logic* (1780).

**Condorcet, Marie Jean** (1743-1794). Born at Ribemont, France, he committed suicide in prison at Bourg-la-Reine. Active in political life during the French Revolution, he was imprisoned after the fall of the government. He was a vigorous *rationalist* and a theoretician of human progress. He opposed the popular view of history and human nature as being static, and felt that progress resulted not from human reflection on history but in the march of science and the uses science makes of history. Key work: *Outline of a Sketch of the Progress of the Human Spirit* (1794).

**Confucius** (551-479 B. C.). Original name: Kung Fu Tse. Born of a poor family in what is now Shangtung, China, he became the Orient's foremost moralist, and in China was for many centuries an object of official worship. He promulgated an ideal conduct of life the basis of which was learning, wisdom, and moral perfection. His doctrine of *reciprocity* in man's relations with his fellow man paralleled, with almost the same words, the Western concept of the Golden Rule. Main work: *Lun Yü* (Analects).

**Conti, Auguste** (1822-1905). Born in Tuscany, this Italian philosopher sought to formulate a kind of fellowship of philosophy — a union of the various schools of thought — by emphasizing their essential points of agreement and minimizing their differences.

**Copernicus, Nicholas** (1473-1543). Born at Thorn, Poland, his proper name was Nicolaus Koppernigk. He became an astronomer and subsequently made discoveries that have had lasting effects on all the philosophical sciences. He proved that the sun was the center of the universe and that without the sun, the world as we know it could not exist. As a result of this, the place and role of man in the universe became infinitely less important than had been thought. Key work: *On the Revolutions of the Stars* (1530).

**Cournot, Antoine Augustin** (1801-1877). French mathematician and philosopher who was born at Gray and died in Paris, and who is best known for his studies in *probability*. He disagreed both with the *positivism* of his day and earlier French *rationalism;* he instead asserted that order and contingency, continuity and discontinuity, are equally real. There is no *essence of truth;* in fact, there is no certainty of truth because *chance* is as equally a force to be considered in evolution as *order* or *purpose*. As long as chance functions, the world cannot be fully explained in scientific terms. From this he concluded that although man cannot attain positive truth, he can, by increasing the probable truth of his statements, *approach* positive truth. Chief works: *Essay on the Theory of Chance and Probability* (1843); *Essay on the Foundations of Knowledge* (1851).

**Cousin, Victor** (1792-1867). Paris born, he lectured at the Sorbonne (1815-1820) until he was suspended for political reasons. At first a *spiritualist,* then an *idealist,* he advocated careful observation and analysis of the facts of conscious life as the basis for metaphysical inquiry. Chief works: *Philosophical Fragments* (1826, 1833, 1838).

**Crates** (c. 350 B. C.). A student of DIOGENES and the teacher of ZENO THE STOIC, he served as a bridge between *cynicism* (the doctrine devoted to ridiculing the pretensions and aspirations of man) and *stoicism* (the philosophy of submission to the laws of nature).

**Cratylus** (c. 450-385 B. C.). An Athenian, he was PLATO's first teacher. He carried the doctrine of the *irreconcilability of opposites* so far that he ultimately renounced the use of spoken language. One of the Platonic dialogues is named after him.

**Crescas, Hasdai** (1340-1410). Jewish philosopher born at Barcelona, Spain, he endured much personal persecution during the first Spanish Inquisition. He was the first European thinker to establish the probability of the existence of an *infinite magnitude* and of *infinite space*, thus paving the way for the modern conception of the universe. Key work: *The Light of God*.

**Croce, Benedetto** (1866-1952). Born near Abruzzi, Italy, he had a long public career as a senator and minister in Italian governments and had a great influence on modern Italian culture. He was an early colleague of GENTILE, but later broke with him on principle. Philosophically, he was concerned with esthetics, logic, ethics and history, but in the final analysis felt that philosophy was nothing but the history of philosophy. However, art is the highest of sciences. Other sciences proceed from single, concrete facts to universal abstractions; whereas art does just the opposite, and it is in coming to grips with the individual and concrete that man best understands reality. Thus, art is man's most valuable tool of knowledge.

**Cudworth, Ralph** (1617-1688). The leading Platonist of his time at Cambridge Univ. in England. He devoted most of his work to refuting the materialism of HOBBES, which he characterized as atheistic. He accepted DESCARTES' type of rationalism and advanced a belief in God as universal reason. Main work: *The True Intellectual System of the Universe*.

**Cusa, Nicholas of** (1401-1464). Born at Cusa, France, his family name was Krebs. He was educated at the Universities of

Heidelberg, Padua and Cologne, and later became a cardinal of the Church (1448) and Bishop of Brixen (1450). He died at Todi. His philosophy was neo-Platonic and mystical, and was highly critical of Aristotelian Scholasticism. He propounded theories of *learned ignorance* and the *concordance of contraries* as explanations for his notions of the proper way to approach truth. Key work: *Doctrine of Ignorance*.

# D

**D'Alembert, Jean Baptiste** (1717-1783). French philosopher and
mathematician who was born at Paris and whose real name
was Jean Baptiste le Rond. He was one of the founders of
*positivism* (i.e. positive knowledge can only be derived from
scientific methods) and had a strong influence on COMTE.
He maintained that there is no such thing as truth; truth
is hypothetical and is merely a result of a psychological compulsion on the part of man to gain certainty of his world.
Knowledge is thus also psychologically generated. Logical
order and historical sequence are the only "truths" able to
be seen in the world, and man has sought to make of these
something other than what they are; that is, he has sought
"truths" where there are, after all, only "facts." D'Alembert
also collaborated with Diderot in compiling the great *French
Encyclopedia* (1751-65), which helped to initiate the Enlightenment. Key work: *Preliminary Discourses* (1751).

**Darwin, Charles Robert** (1809-1882). Born at Shrewsbury, England, he was a biologist whose famous theory of *evolution*
is important to philosophy for the effects it has had on
speculations about the nature of man. After many years
of careful study, he attempted to show that higher species
had come into existence as a result of the gradual transformation of lower species; and that the process of transformation could be explained through the selective effect of
the natural environment upon organisms. He thus concluded
that the principles of *natural selection* and *survival of the*

51

*fittest* govern all life. These theories confirmed to some degree the early philosophies of *universal naturalism,* and also spawned various modern doctrines of *universal organism.* Key work: *On the Origin of the Species* (1859).

**Dawes Hicks, George** (1862-1941). An English thinker born at Shrewsbury, he was for many years a professor of philosophy at University College in London (1904-1928). Mainly concerned with the theory of knowledge, he developed a distinctive doctrine which he called *critical realism.* The essence of this doctrine is that objects exist independently of our knowing them and that what we are immediately aware of about any object is only a part of the content of that object.

**Delboeuf, Joseph Remi Leopold** (1831-1896). Belgian philosopher who was born and died at Liege. He is known mainly for his invention of the philosophy of *psychophysics* (a combination of metaphysics and psychology) which sought to resolve the age-old problem of the relationship between mind and body. Key works: *Introduction to the Philosophy of Logic* (1860); *Essay on Scientific Logic* (1875).

**Democritus** (c. 460-360 B. C.). From Abdera, he was one of the first of the ancient Greek philosophers and developed the first *materialistic* philosophy of nature. He taught that all substance consists of atoms (indivisible and imperceptibly small particles). The variety of atomic forms corresponds to, and explains, the variety of material qualities; the finest, smoothest and most agile atoms constitute the human mind. His theory of knowledge, though by modern standards primitive, was quite sophisticated for his day. He explained perception as an *emanation* of tiny copies of sensible things, which, through their impact on the atoms of the mind, leave impressions that are responsible for the facts of memory. Key work: *The World Order in Detail.*

**De Morgan, Augustus** (1806-1871). English logician who was born in India and who taught at University College in London (1836-1866). His mathematical principles were similar to those of BOOLE, but he is most noteworthy as the founder of the *logic of relations* and as the developer of the *algebra of logic* (which reconstructed the logic of ARISTOTLE upon a mathematical basis). Main work: *Formal Logic* (1847).

**De Sanctis, Francesco** (1817-1883). Born at Morra, Italy, he was an active revolutionary who fought for the unification of Italy (1848) and was imprisoned for four years. Upon his release, and after he had become an authority in the philosophy of Hegel, he became a professor of philosophy at Zurich, Switzerland. He later became Minister of Public Education in Italy (1861) and a professor of literature and philosophy at the Univ. of Naples (1871). His chief contribution to philosophy was in aesthetics, as an advocate of the doctrine of *formalism*. He claimed that *form* alone, rather than the co-existence of form and substance, was the essence of art. He opposed psychological approaches to the arts and insisted upon formal analyses. Key works: *Critical Essays* (1870-71); *New Critical Essays* (1872).

**Descartes, René** (1596-1650). Born at La Haye, France. After completing his formal education at the Jesuit College at Le Flèche, he spent nine years (1612-1621) in travel and military service. The remainder of his life was devoted to study and writing. He died in Sweden, where he had gone to tutor Queen Christiana. Regarded as one of the founders of modern epistemology, he was the first philosopher to bring mathematical methods to bear on speculative thought. He began by asserting that everything that could not *immediately* pass his criterion of truth (i.e. the clearness and distinctness of ideas) was worthy of doubt. Anything that could pass this test was to be considered self-evident. From self-evident truths, he was able to deduce other truths which logically followed from them. The first self-evident truth to be discovered, according to him, is that of the *thinking self*. Since the fact that he thought was the clearest and most distinct idea he could have, he could not doubt that he existed. (This intuition was enunciated in his famous *Cogito, ergo sum;* "I think, therefore I am"). The other truth that he recognized immediately according to his criterion was God, and he gave a *mathematical proof* for the existence of God (the existence of a divine and perfect being [God]) is comprised of and evident by the very idea of such an existence, just as the equality of the three angles of a triangle to two right angles is comprised of and evident by the idea of a triangle). From these two clear and distinct ideas, he developed a highly elaborate system of thought that spread throughout all divisions of philosophy. His impact on the subsequent history of philosophy was considerable. Chief work: *Discourse on Method*.

**Deussen, Paul** (1845-1919). Born at Oberdreis, Germany, he developed a system of thought that drew heavily from KANT's *idealism,* SCHOPENHAUER's *pessimism,* and the Hindu doctrine of the *world soul* as the combined essence of all individual souls. Key work: *History of Philosophy* (1917).

**Deustua, Alejandro** (1849-1945). Born at Huancayo, Peru. He taught philosophy at Univ. of San Marcos in Lima for many years. His philosophy was based on an esthetic consideration of freedom in conjunction with Hegelian dialectic (analysis, antithesis, synthesis). There are two kinds of freedom, *static* (the cosmic order) and *dynamic* (human creativity). Oppose these dialectically and the result is the world as we experience it through our consciousness. Main work: *The Ideas of Order and Freedom in the History of Human Thought* (1917-22).

**Dewey, John** (1859-1952). Born at Burlington, Vermont, he became one of the foremost American philosophers and had a long career as a teacher, first at the Univ. of Michigan, then at Chicago, then at Columbia Univ. His metaphysics concluded that the world has no ultimate purpose or meaning; his ethics, that what is right is simply and only what will work best in the relative context of a meaningless world; and his conception of the chief end of man, not the fellowship of God, not moral virtue, but sensate well-being. He is probably most important for his development of the logical theory of *instrumentalism* (that form of *pragmatism* that emphasized the efficacy of ideas used as intellectual tools for the solution of problems as long as the ideas were constantly tested for their validity). He made *inquiry*, rather than truth or knowledge, the essence of logic. Relating all philosophy to practical aims, he identified knowledge with action and declared that any philosophy that was not applicable to the affairs of man had no point. To him, "intelligent action" was the fruit of philosophy. Main works: *Reconstruction in Philosophy* (1920); *Human Nature and Conduct* (1922); *Experience and Nature* (1925); *Art as Experience* (1933); *Logic: The Theory of Inquiry* (1939).

**Diderot, Denis** (1713-1784). As an editor with D'ALEMBERT of the *French Encyclopedia* (1751-65), he had a far-reaching influence on the Enlightenment. Beginning as a *deist* (i.e. God exists, but has no relation to the world), he concluded his life as a *pantheist* (i.e. God is totally in nature). He advocated *skepticism* in opposition to dogmatism and held that nothing could be taken as absolutely true for all time. Since *change* is the fundamental principle of life — or so our sense experience tells us — truth must, like everything else, be subject to change.

**Dilthey, Wilhelm** (1833-1911). This German historian of philosophy developed a new methodology for the study of society and culture. He was the founder of *Lebensphilosophie* (*Phi-*

*losophy of Manners*), but his main contribution came from his comprehensive research as a biographical historian of intellectual development. He described life as a *series of experiences,* all of which bear an inner relation to one another. Every individual experience is an *historic episode* that refers to a self, and the combination of all the experiences of an individual constitutes the total mind of that individual. Likewise, the sum of all experiences in history constitutes the whole of life, or the *total world mind.* This total world mind, since it binds all life together, has unity —it is the real *cosmic spirit.* Man can comprehend the cosmic spirit by virtue of the coherent unity of his consciousness. Thus, again, history is at the center of any cognition of the world.

**Diogenes** (c. 412-323 B. C.). From Sinope, on the Black Sea, he became a student of ANTISTHENES and a leading exponent of ancient *cynicism.* His cynicism was more of a practice than a doctrine. He was an independent thinker and an individualist who devoted his life, as it were, to "looking for an honest man." (He is not to be confused with Diogenes Laertes, a third century biographer of Greek philosophy).

**Drews, Arthur** (1865-1935). German thinker born at Uetersen and educated at the Universities of Munich, Berlin, Heidelberg and Halle. Although he was an important philosopher during his time — mainly as a critic and interpreter of other philosophies — his principal fame derives from his book *The Legend of Peter,* in which he attacked the historical accuracy of the New Testament and set the stage for a whole new approach to Biblical analysis.

**Driesch, Hans** (1867-1940). German biologist who brought his organic theories into the study of philosophy. He asserted that every organism has its own essence; being is therefore *individual,* and cannot be defined as universal. Main work: *Philosophy of the Organism* (1912).

56

**Ducasse, Curt John** (1881-   ). An American philosopher who was born in France. He developed the doctrine of *semanticism* (i.e. philosophy should deal primarily with semantics and the linguistic analysis of value terms). As for metaphysical questions, he subscribes to the doctrine of *metempsychosis* (which originated with Pythagoras and is similar to the Buddhist theory of the *transmigration of souls;* i.e. on death, the soul leaves the body and enters the body of another living creature). Key work: *Nature, Mind and Death* (1951).

**Dühring, Eugen Karl** (1833-1901). Born in Berlin, he originally embarked upon a legal career but turned to philosophy when he lost his eyesight. He advanced a doctrine of *materialistic heroism* — a stoic acceptance of a world that is basically evil. He also advocated a worldwide religion of ethics to overcome what he felt were the progress-hindering elements in the various theological creeds of the world. Key works: *Natural Dialectic* (1865); *Logic and the Theory of Knowledge* (1905).

**Duns Scotus, John** (c. 1266-1308). Born most likely at Maxton in Scotland. A Franciscan monk, he was educated at Oxford and the Univ. of Paris. He taught theology at Oxford (1300-1302) and at Paris (1303), and died at Cologne. He is most noteworthy for his criticism of the views of AUGUSTINE and AQUINAS. Instead of matter and form, he posited the extremely modern concept of *haecceity* (the singular, undefinable quality of ultimate reality) and *quiddity* (the whatness of things). He declared that it was not reality that was limited, but the human intellect. His form of realism was antagonistic to Scholastic philosophy and he suffered great personal ridicule as a result. Key work: *First Principles.*

**Durkheim, Emile** (1858-1917). French sociologist who employed the concepts of *positivism* (i.e. the highest form of knowledge consists in simple descriptions of things) to bring a new objective dimension to sociology. Main work: *The Rules of Sociological Method.*

# E

**Eckhardt, Meister** (1260-1327). Basically a theologian, this Ger-man-born Dominican received his doctorate in theology at the Univ. of Paris (1302). Mystical and complex, his thought contains elements of practically all the noteworthy schools of the Middle Ages. Accused of *pantheism* and other heresies, he was the subject of a famous trial (1326). He subsequently admitted and renounced his errors, but even after his death his thought continued to be condemned. Chief work: *Opus Tripartitum.*

**Edwards, Jonathan** (1703-1758). American theologian who was born in Connecticut and who has philosophical importance because of the aesthetic foundations of his highly formalized theology. Although he began as a student of philosophy, admiring especially LOCKE and CUDWORTH, he quickly lost interest in abstract speculation and devoted his life to both formal theology, through his writing, and to practical applica-tion of his ideals, through the ministry and missionary work. Was elected President (1757) of what is now Princeton Univ. Key work: *On the Freedom of Will* (1874).

**Ehrenfels, Maria Christian** (1859-1932). As one of the leaders of the Brentano School, his thought was psychology-oriented. He affirmed the assertion that the fundamental factor in valuation and judgment was desire, and traced the way in which emotional motivations generate values. He had a major influence upon the analytic approach to ethics and value theory. Main works: *System der Werktheorie* (1897); *Sexualethik* (1907).

**Einstein, Albert** (1879-1955). German born scientist and discoverer of the Theory of Relativity, which has had important implications for philosophy. His *Special Theory of Relativity* enforced a change in the classical conceptions of *time* and *space*: time and space are not independent of each other and do not exist as co-equal, absolute constituents of the universe; rather, they are dependent entities that exist in a close relationship. In their place as absolute constituents of the universe, he assigned the concept of *magnitude,* which in a way is a compound of time and space. His *General Theory of Relativity* upset some classical notions about knowledge. It implied that whatever we are able to comprehend through the immediate senses we shall regard as true, and no theory can put out of existence that which our senses teach us is fact. However, only a small portion of the world can be known by the senses; whatever happens beyond them must be deduced by *reasoned reflection.* Key works: *The General Theory of Relativity* (1916); *The World As I See It* (1953).

**Emerson, Ralph Waldo** (1803-1882). American thinker and essayist, he was born at Boston and died at Concord, New Hampshire. A *transcendentalist,* his principal philosophical question was with respect to the relationship of man to the universe. His answer consisted in his linking the *human soul* to a *World Soul.* He held that all men are vital parts of the vast organism of mankind — mankind is meant to be *one,* and all men, through what he called the basic instinct for fellowship, strive toward recognition of the Universal Soul which merges all individual souls into one. So then, man's fundamental function in life should be to seek a transcendental communion of souls. By so doing, his ethical and moral compulsions are set out for him to follow. Key work: *Essays.*

60

**Empedocles** (c. 490-430 B. C.). He was from Agrigentum on the south coast of Sicily. He tried to reconcile the doctrine of the *permanence of being* (Eleatics) with the doctrine of *change and motion* (as advanced by HERACLITUS). He originated and taught the doctrine of *four elements* (i.e. the universe is permanently constituted of the elements of air, earth, fire and water, and all things derive their existence from the mixing of these). He also taught that love and hate were the causes of motion and were thus responsible for the mixing of the elements (love causing the combining of things, hate their separation).

**Engels, Friedrich** (1820-1895). Born at Barmen, Germany, he is best known for his collaboration and support of MARX. He established the economic and political doctrine of *dialectical materialism* by means of his editing and completing the last two volumes of Marx's *Kapital*. He also tried to construct a rationalistic morality to support the doctrines of communism, claiming that the most durable elements of modern morality are to be found in the proletarian (working class) movement. Key work: *On the Situation of the Working Class* (1845).

**Epictetus** (c. 60-110 A. D.). A *stoic* philosopher born in Asia Minor who, after being freed from Roman slavery, established a school in Epirus. He is noteworthy for his famous *Encheridion,* a transcription by one of his pupils of his numerous lectures and discourses that contains sharp observations on human behavior and pithy comments on ethical questions. He taught that reason governed the world and was identical with God.

**Epicurus** (341-270 B. C.). A native of Samos and founder of the *Epicurean* School in Athens (306 B. C.). He taught that pleasure and happiness are the natural ends of life. Contrary to later misinterpretations, he did not advocate the bold pursuit of pleasure for its own sake, but only those pleasures that are consistent with reason and moderation. Joys of the mind are superior to pleasures of the body. His concept of nature mainly followed the *atomism* of DEMOCRITUS, though he disavowed determinism and established a doctrine of *cosmic chance* (i.e. an element of *chance* enters into the atoms' motions and causes deviations, thus accounting for both natural and psychic disorders). Key work: *On Nature.*

**Erasmus, Desiderius** (1466-1536). Dutch religious philosopher who was born at Rotterdam. Although deeply religious, he fought against all forms of religious fanaticism and advocated *reason* as the road to the true enlightenment that would result in moral righteousness. The central theme of his philosophy was moral, and is best stated in his own words: "The religion consists in adherence to the simplicity of Christ." Although he did not repudiate the divinity of Christ, he felt that the moral example represented by Christ was the most cogent aspect of Christ's nature for man to emulate. Key work: *In Praise of Folly* (1509).

**Erdmann, Benno** (1851-1921). German philosopher and teacher who was strongly steeped in the *critical idealism* of KANT. He claimed that the *real* world exists in the mind, while the data of the senses present us with only the *apparent* world. Key works: *Studies in Logic* (1878); *The Theory of Apperception* (1886).

**Erigena, Johannes Scotus** (c. 815-877). An Irish-born monk, he became a teacher in France at the court of Charles the Bald, son of Charlemagne. He asserted that philosophy was identical with religion and held to a concept of God working in nature in *four forms* (uncreated creator; created creator; created non-creator; uncreated non-creator). He declined to speculate on God's characteristics or attributes but declared that "God is not a what, but a that." Through his scholar-

62

ship, he was instrumental in reviving philosophical thought, which was dormant after the death of BOETHIUS, in Western Europe.

**Eucken, Rudolph** (1846-1926). Born at Aurich, he was a German historian of philosophy and Nobel Prize winner (1908). Strongly *spiritualistic* and *idealistic,* he repudiated various philosophies that emphasized the importance of the mind (*positivism, materialism,* etc.) and attempted to demonstrate, especially through history, that spiritual life — or a sort of *universal motion* that existed in all things — was the true cause of relationships and phenomena in the natural world. He coined the term *syntagma* to characterize his elaborate philosophy. Key work: *The Life of the Spirit* (1888).

**Euclid** (c. 335-275 B. C.). Living during the reign of Ptolemy I in Egypt, he resided at Alexandria and developed a system of mathematics that is the basis of both ancient and modern mathematical systems. He is important to philosophy for his invention of the mathematical method of reasoning. Chief work: *Stoicheia* (*The Elements*).

**Euclid of Megara** (c. 450-375 B. C.). Founder of the *Megaran* school of Greek philosophy, he identified the *Good* with the *One* and claimed the *Many* to be unreal, merely a meaningless concept and not worthy of consideration in speculating about the causes of things.

# F

**Fechner, Gustav Theodor** (1801-1887). He was born in Lusatia, in Germany, and educated at the Univ. of Leipzig. Although a physicist trained in practical methods of investigation, he expounded a philosophy much like that of BERKELEY, consisting of a pure, objective *idealism*. With SCHELLING as his spiritual guide, he held that all things exist only in consciousness; that there are no such things as universal substances or things-in-themselves but that everything which exists does so within the context of a kind of universal soul. As humans, we all have at least partial access to this consciousness (soul), while God, as the highest in the order of things, has total and infinite access. Main work: *Elements of Psycho-Physics* (1860).

**Feuerbach, Ludwig Andreas** (1804-1872). Born at Landshut, he was one of the earliest German thinkers manifesting a trend toward *materialism* in the 19th century. Yet he felt materialism did not constitute the best means of reaching complete truth, so he turned to anthropological studies and concluded that God was only an idea formed by man to satisfy man's longing for reconciling the contradictions of life. He rejected idealism flatly, asserting that man was nothing without the world of objects with which he was connected. He defined existence as the abundance of sensual relations, and sensuality as the criterion of existence (I feel, therefore I exist). Key work: *The Essence of Christianity* (1841).

65

**Fichte, Johann Gottlieb** (1762-1814). German thinker born at Rammenan, his early studies were in theology. After becoming friendly with KANT and infused with his thought, he began to write on philosophy. His thought was centered on a fervent espousal of Kant's notion of *practical reason.* He assumed *consciousness* to be the core about which the universe turns (i.e. we all live in our own worlds, which are connected through a universal consciousness brought into being by an ultimate cause). His philosophy is best characterized as *subjective idealism* (i.e. the understanding of the origin and nature of *consciousness* is the key to all problems, and it is the *ego* that is the point at which the Absolute emerges in individual consciousness). He lectured widely throughout Germany, and his more popular works were instrumental in initiating the German uprising against the Napoleonic occupation. Major work: *Science of Knowledge.*

**Ficino, Marsilio** (1433-1499). Born in Florence, he became the main spokesman for Platonism in the Italian Renaissance. His thought combined neo-Platonic metaphysics and Augustinian theology with many new ideas of his own. He propounded a hierarchical system of the universe (God, Angelic Mind, Soul, Quality, Body). He considered man to be at the center of the universe and human life as an eternal ascent of the soul towards God. Major work: *Platonic Theology* (1482).

**Fiedler, Conrad** (1841-1895). Born into a prosperous family in Saxony, he was educated at Heidelberg for a career in law. However, he soon became interested in art and the philosophy of art. He was plainly the source of much of CROCE's teaching on the relation between intuition and expression and on the ultimate nature of art as a source of knowledge. Fiedler thought of art as a complement of science in the pursuit of *Erkenntnis* (knowledge of the world) and regarded the aesthetic side of art as trivial in comparison. Key works: *Reality and Art; Origin of Artistic Activity.*

**Filmer, Robert** (c. 1595-1653). Born in Kent, England, and educated at Cambridge Univ., he became noteworthy as a political philosopher because of his unusual efforts to preserve traditional values — especially the doctrine of the *divine right of kings* — at a time when unreasonable traditions were being attacked. He purported to prove that such doctrine was authorized by the Bible, claiming that the right of inheritance, as reflected in the Old Testament, was divinely bestowed on the Hebrew patriarchs, and that the notion of the divine right of kings was nothing but a modern manifestation of the biblical notion of the right of inheritance. Key work: *Patriarcha, Or the Natural Power of Kings Asserted* (1680).

**Fischer, Ernst Kuno** (1824-1907). Born at Sanderwalde, he is important as one of the eminent German historians of philosophy. He helped to initiate a revival of the philosophy of KANT in opposition to the growing *materialism* of the late 19th century in Germany. Main work: *System of Logic and Metaphysics.*

**Fiske, John** (1842-1901). Best known for his historical studies of the American colonial period, he was also a professor of philosophy at Harvard who pioneered in studies of evolutionary theories. He was *theistic* in his point of view. Main work: *Outlines of a Cosmic Philosophy,* 2 vols. (1874).

**Flügel, Otto** (1842-1914). German theological thinker mainly known to philosophy for his insistence that the speculations of philosophical probabilities must depend upon the revelations of theological certainties. Key work: *Materialism* (1865).

**Fourier, François** (1772-1837). Born at Besançon, France, he was a political and economic philosopher who sought to replace the profit system with a system similar to communism. He felt that the profit system by nature contained too many built-in abusive elements and that it prevented human progress because it engendered unethical practices. He devised a utopian plan whereby *phalanges,* or cooperative communities, would be established and labor would be divided among all the members. After gaining many adherents both in Europe and in the U.S. during the first half of the 19th century, Fourierism died out — mainly because of its impracticality. Key works: *Treatise on an Agricultural Society* (1822); *The New Industrial and Social World* (1829).

**Frege, Gottlob** (1848-1925). German logician who taught at the Univ. of Jena (1879-1918). His work had great significance in the development of *symbolic logic;* he also developed an arithmetic based on the rules of logic. He believed that logic (how we reason), not the theory of knowledge (how we know), is the point of departure for philosophy generally. Key work: *Arithmetic and Logic* (1948).

**Fries, Jakob Friedrich** (1773-1843). German thinker whose main contribution to philosophy lay in his continuation of KANT's work on reason and his efforts to mould philosophy into an exact science. He mixed Kantian metaphysics with Platonic idealism and concluded that human minds are capable of apprehending directly the transcendental reality of the ideas by means of "feeling" (*Ahnung*). Main work: *New or Anthropological Criticism of Reason.*

# G

**Gabirol, Solomon ibn.** See AVICEBRON.

**Galilei, Galileo** (1564-1642). Born at Pisa, Italy, this astronomer-physicist is known mainly for his discoveries in mechanics and space; he is also memorable for his spirited defense of COPERNICUS' theory of the solar system. He is important to philosophy because of the way he used the experimental method in conjunction with mathematical calculation, a system that has influenced many subsequent thinkers.

**Gassendi, Pierre** (1592-1655). A Catholic priest who was born at Provence, France. He was at one time Canon of Dijon; later became a professor of mathematics at the Royal College of Paris (1645). He was a leading opponent of the thought of DESCARTES, and although his theological views were orthodox, he revived and championed the *materialistic atomism* of EPICURUS as a semi-scientific explanation of the working of the natural world. Key work: *Objections,* to Descartes' *Meditations* (1642).

**Gentile, Giovanni** (1875-1944). Born in Sicily, he became the official philosopher of Italian Fascism. After professorships of philosophy at the Universities of Palermo (1907-14) and Pisa (1915-21), he became Mussolini's Minister of Public Education (1922) and effected a dictatorial reform of Italy's school system. On the speculative plane, he developed the doctrine of *actualism* (i.e. pure act is identical with the spirit

69

and is reality itself; reality is nothing but the relationship between a subject's spirit and the objective, spiritless phenomena of the world; the action of this relationship defines the world). On the more practical level, he propounded the doctrine of the *ethic state* (to which the individual must be totally sacrificed). Chief works: *General Theory of the Spirit as Pure Act* (1916); *Logic as Theory of Knowledge* (1917).

**Gersonides** (1288-1340). Born Levi ben Gerson at Languedoc in the south of France, he was an astronomer as well as a philosopher. His thought was strongly forged by Aristotelianism. His theory of the soul teaches that *passive* or *material intellect* is only a potentiality for developing pure thought which is accomplished through the Universal Active Intellect (God). It is in this way that God manifests himself in the world. The possession of an active intellect is, according to him, a condition of immortality. Key work: *The War of God.*

**Geulincx, Arnold** (1624-1669). Born a Catholic at Antwerp, Belgium, he taught first at the Univ. of Louvain. He then converted to Calvinism and emigrated to Holland. He was influenced by DESCARTES, but became dissatisfied with the Cartesian solution of the *mind-body* problem. As a result, he developed the doctrine of *occasionalism* (i.e. the interaction between mind and body is impossible, but God generates bodily motions on the occasion of each mental process). Main works: *Ethics* (1655); *Metaphysics* (1665).

**Geyser, Joseph** (1863-1948). Born at Erkelenz, Germany, he was a leader of Catholic metaphysical thought in Europe. He taught at the Universities of Freiburg and Munich, where he criticized *materialistic* tendencies in psychology and espoused Aristotelian concepts about the causes of things. Key work: *Foundations of Empirical Psychology* (1902).

**Gilson, Etienne** (1884–   ). A French-born Catholic, he is principally an historian and an interpreter of the philosophy of AQUINAS. He repudiates efforts to systematize and scientize philosophy and rejects the identification of Thomistic philosophy with Scholasticism. He asserts instead that systematization by its nature tends to abolish philosophy, whereas Thomism, by its permanent yet modifiable truths, keeps philosophy and the spirit of inquiry alive. Key work: *God and Philosophy* (1941).

**Gioberti, Vincenzo** (1801-1852). Born at Turin, Italy, he became a priest (1825) but was exiled to Paris (1833) because of his liberal views. Later he returned to Italy (1848) and served as a minister and ambassador. His philosophy tackled the problem of the relation between the senses and the intellect. He asserted that *universal spirit* becomes *individual* through its own creation; thus, the source of individuality is divine, not subjective. Moreover, individuality returns to universality when it is able to rise from a state of sensibility to a state of intelligibility. While his method relied upon intuitive faith in the Absolute, it used a purely philosophical conception of the universe: essence creates existence, and existence returns to essence. Key work: *New Knowledge of the Origin of Ideas* (1829).

**Gobineau, Joseph Arthur** (1816-1882). Born near Paris, this French reactionary philosopher promoted the idea of the superiority of the "Nordic" race. Ignored in his own country, he found acceptance for his views in Germany and became a fanatical champion of the "superiority" of Germans over all other peoples. Not a little of later Nazi theory was gleaned directly from Gobineau's racist doctrines.

**Goblot, Edmond** (1858-1935). French philosopher who espoused the *rationalism* of COMTE and rejected the *intuitionism* of BERGSON. Concerned mainly with religion, he favored the scientific approach and preferred the facts of reason to what he regarded as the fictions of revelation. Key work: *The True, the Intelligible, the Real* (1922).

**Gödel, Kurt** (1906-   ). Austrian logician and mathematician educated at Vienna. Best known to philosophy for his arithmetization of syntax.

**Goodman, Nelson** (1906-   ). American philosopher, he was born in Massachusetts and has been for many years a professor of philosophy at the Univ. of Pennsylvania. He is important mainly for his metaphysical views. A *nominalist,* he rejects the conception of the universe as a structure of ideas; rather, he sees the world as constituted of *patterns of various elementary components of experience* and feels that the function of philosophy is to give — based on experience — precise descriptions of the structure of the world through definitions that exhibit these patterns of experience. Key work: *The Structure of Experience* (1951).

**Gorgias** (c. 480-375 B. C.). Ancient rhetorician, orator and philosopher; born in Sicily. Was a leader of the *Sophist* school of Greek philosophy (which sought to popularize knowledge and make it available and more readily comprehensible through an argumentative method of defense and opposition. Sophists were stigmatized by ARISTOTLE as a group of opportunistic thinkers who, for the sake of money or other earthly considerations, would teach falsehoods).

**Grabmann, Martin** (1875-1949). German historian of medieval philosophy and a specialist on the authenticity and chronology of the works of AQUINAS. Key work: *The Scholastic Method* (1911).

**Green, Thomas Hill** (1836-1882). Long a celebrated professor of moral philosophy at Oxford, he was an *idealist* in the HEGEL

72

mould and repudiated the utilitarianism fashionable in his time. He flatly rejected the assumption that sensations are the raw material of knowledge, and argued that consciousness is self-distinguishing and acts as a connective agent between the senses and the Absolute to avail us of knowledge. Without this, we would not think but would only feel. Thus, since we can think and are able to distinguish ourselves as part of a larger whole to which we are related, that relation and that whole cannot be created by the merely finite self but must be the creation of something larger; namely, the Absolute. Main work: *Prolegomena to Ethics* (1883).

**Grotius, Hugo** (1583-1645). Dutch jurist born at Delft. As a legal philosopher, he presented a theory of natural law based largely on *stoicism* and Roman Law. He distinguished between natural rights (inviolable and permanent) and human rights (changeable and developing), and insisted that human legal systems could not be valid without first affirming the supreme authority of natural law. Key work: *The Laws of Peace* (1625).

**Guyau, Jean Marie** (1854-1888). French philosopher born at Laval. He was an *idealist* who advanced the doctrine of *moral necessity* (i.e. *altruism* is a natural instinct rather than an acquired characteristic; as a result, a moral compunction *to do and act right* is integrally built into man's power *to do and act*). Key work: *Toward a Philosophy* (1881).

# H

**Haeberlin, Paul** (1878-1961). Swiss-born, he was for many years a professor of philosophy at the Univ. of Basel. A religion-oriented philosopher, he maintained that because life and existence were by their nature problematical, so too was knowledge, which emanated from life. He characterized the human mind as a kind of constant protest against this fact, which remains a mystery to man but is not a mystery to God, since God is responsible for its creation. The function of philosophy, then, is to help man to obtain knowledge of his real situation; however, without a religious affirmation of the cause of his situation, philosophy is wasted on man. A form of *existentialism,* his thought is best described as a God-centered *transcendental idealism.* Main work: *The Essence of Philosophy* (1934).

**Haeckel, Ernst Heinrich** (1834-1919). German biologist and philosopher, born at Potsdam. His early espousal of the theories of DARWIN led him to build upon the concept of *evolution* a doctrine of *material monism* (i.e. matter is the one fundamental reality; thus, the universe is a single material substance). He believed in the *singularity* of essence in both the organic and the inorganic, and rejected revealed religions and their ideas of God. Main work: *The Riddle of the Universe* (1904).

**Halevi, Judah** (c. 1080-1140). Jewish poet and philosopher, born at Toledo, Spain. His main work, *Kuzari,* was a skillful exaltation of Judaism that endeavored to show the insufficiency of philosophy and the superiority of the truths of revealed religion to those arrived at by logic.

**Hamann, Johann Georg** (1730-1788). A contemporary and friend of KANT who criticized the latter's critical philosophy as an unsuccessful attempt to make reason independent of all tradition, accepted beliefs and experience. He insisted that no attempt to explain the mechanism of reasoning can equal belief, which he regarded as the foundation of all knowledge. Key work: *Metacritique* (1782).

**Hamelin, Octave** (1856-1907). French idealist philosopher, he was born at Lyon and died at Huclat. He was strongly influenced by KANT and HEGEL, and attempted to explain the process of existence by elaborating his own system of Kantian categories and then synthesizing the opposites of each category by means of the Hegelian dialectic. To him, the concept of *relation* was the primary category of existence, and it was this that made synthesis possible. For instance, number — a secondary category of existence — is the synthesis of two opposites: plurality and unity. As in this synthesis, all things in nature could be unified through similar syntheses, and it was the principle of relation that made such synthesization possible (i.e. all things exist in relation to one another). Key work: *Essay on the Principal Elements of Representation* (1907).

**Hamilton, William** (1788-1856). Scottish thinker born in Glasgow, he taught philosophy for many years at the Univ. of Glasgow. Problems in logic and metaphysics were his main concern; his principal works were aimed at justifying his central theory that knowledge presents itself immediately to consciousness and not through any intermediary such as the objective world. Key work: *Lectures on Metaphysics and Logic,* 4 vol. (1859-60).

**Han Fei** (c. 280-233 B.C.). A disciple of HSÜN CHING and the foremost Chinese philosopher of law. He committed suicide because, as an unofficial adviser to a contemporary ruler, he aroused the jealousy of the ruler's leading minister. His philosophy was directed to problems of government and statecraft, and he advanced views similar to those of much later British utilitarian philosophers.

**Hannequin, Arthur Edouard** (1856-1905). French scientific philosopher who, influenced by the *atomism* of such ancient Greeks as DEMOCRITUS, developed the doctrine of *atomistic synthesis* (i.e. a form of analysis that tries to make intelligible the motion of atoms by a synthesis of their number and continuity) as a method of understanding reality. To him, the motion of atoms is the first cause of things and, therefore, constitutes reality; hence, the understanding of reality implies the understanding of this motion. However, this motion consists of unintelligible and contrary atoms; therefore, a synthesis is required — through the mind — to unify the diversity of atoms and make them intelligible. By making them intelligible, the mind comes to grips with the motion, which is to say, with reality. Main work: *Critique on the Atomic Hypothesis in Contemporary Science* (1895).

**Harrison, Frederic** (1831-1923). English philosopher and jurist, he was born in London, was a follower of COMTE, and became the leader of English *positivism*. His principal contention was that philosophy should be based on science rather than on metaphysics. He had considerable influence on RUSSELL and WHITEHEAD. Key work: *The Meaning of History* (1862).

**Hartley, David** (1705-1757). English thinker, noted as the founder of the *associationist* school of psychology. His theory of the *association of ideas* influenced such utilitarians as BENTHAM and MILL.

**77**

**Hartmann, Karl Eduard von** (1842-1906). Born in Berlin, he was originally an officer in the Prussian army but was forced to abandon the military life due to a disabling disease. He turned to philosophy, taking from the *blind will* of SCHOPEN-HAUER and the *absolute spirit* of HEGEL to postulate a concept of *unconsciousness* that was at once unique and complex. He called the unconscious the *thing-in-itself* — the origin of the cosmic order and of the mental life of the individual — and called his system *transcendental realism*. Main work: *Philosophy of the Unconscious* (1869).

**Hartmann, Nikolai** (1882-1950). Born and educated at Riga in Tsarist Russia, he emigrated to Germany and became a citizen of that country. Hartmann's thought begins in the assertion that no one starts with his own thinking, but rather meets an historically conditioned situation in which ideas and problems have already been developed by previous thinkers. Because of this, the various sciences of philosophy (metaphysics, ethics, logic, etc.) can offer only partial solutions to the problems of man, since all ideas are subject to historical change and nothing is permanent except, perhaps, the *structure of ideas*. It is to this structure that philosophy should address itself. Main works: *Ethics* (1922); *The Philosophy of German Idealism,* Vol. I and II (1923-29).

**Hegel, Georg Wilhelm Friedrich** (1770-1831). Born at Stuttgart, Germany, he studied philosophy and theology at Tübingen (1788-93); was a tutor in Switzerland and at Frankfort (1795-1800); taught philosophy at the Univ. of Jena (1801-06); was forced to leave when Napoleon invaded; went to Bamberg, where he remained two years as a newspaper editor (1806-08); then became director of the gymnasium at Nürnberg (1809-16); spent two further years as a professor of philosophy at Heidelberg (1816-18); finally, went to the Univ. of Berlin, where he succeeded FICHTE. Hegel's philosophy can be divided into two realms of significance —

his *doctrine* and his *method* — although the two are held to be logically inseparable (i.e. the method is precisely the formulation of the doctrine; the doctrine is precisely the detailed expression of the method — one does not exist without the other). The Hegelian method is known as *dialectic*. In its formal arrangement, it consists of a triad of *thesis, antithesis,* and *synthesis* (i.e. a statement about a thing; a contrary statement about the same thing; and a third statement synthesizing the first two and, ideally, out of the first two making a third that demonstrates a positive insight into the thing). However, he was hardly ever this formal, and used the triad only to exploit the possibilities of logic in attaining to knowledge. He used the method to demonstrate that the logical structure is *in* everything, that this structure is constituted of contraries, and that out of the contraries comes real or valid knowledge. The dialectic method is everywhere grounded in the system; the successful working of the dialectic, therefore, exhibits the system and the structure of it. However, dialectical analysis is only possible within systems that are factual (i.e. constituted by statements of possibility grounded in fact) and not in abstract systems. Hence, the principle of *contrariety,* not the principle of *contradiction,* is the subject of dialectical analysis. The method, then, is the delineation of systems that are real, so that a successful dialectic results in a demonstration of reality. Which brings us to Hegel's doctrine. The final statement of a successful dialectic is reality, or what he called the *Absolute Idea* (Hegel's concept of the ultimate reality and the truth of being). Since the dialectic is rooted in fact, and since the highest result of the dialectic is Absolute Idea, then Absolute Idea is fact. He claimed that the combination of his method with his doctrine laid open the possibility of definite knowledge of what previously had only been conceived or guessed at: the Ultimate. The human mind, since it can invent so sublime a method as the dialectic to arrive at a clear knowledge of the Absolute Spirit (another term for Absolute Idea), must be a manifestation of the same spirit because of its ability to conceive and work out so perfect a method. He also felt that the world worked in an identical dialectical progression. His concept of history, in other words, was of history as a dialectic. To him, history is nothing else but the movement of thought — the integration of thesis and antithesis into synthesis which, on its part, provokes a new antithesis (negation) with which it becomes integrated into a new synthesis, and so on. These succeeding syntheses will eventually bring the world to reason, he claimed. To put it another way, history is nothing but the constant flow of things and their contraries, new things and their new contraries, etc., and it is the recognition of this dialectical progression that affords us true knowledge of the world. Thus, the world, as all things, can be understood through and in the dialectic, of which it and they are a part. Ultimately, dialectic is the Absolute Idea, or the Absolute Spirit. See: *Collected Works* (1832-40).

**Heidegger, Martin** (1889-   ). German metaphysical thinker, born at Baden, who for several decades was a professor of philosophy at the Univ. of Freiburg. Basically concerned with *being* and *existence,* he is to a large degree the founder of modern *existentialism.* While his method of presenting his philosophy is extremely abstract, complex and obscure, the philosophy itself is comprehensible and, in its psychological orientation, quite sensible. It is based upon the very real, problematical condition of man in the world and the psychological relation of man to his condition. His study of *being,* with a view to explaining man's condition, is based primarily on the emotions. Instead of postulating traditional concepts (*soul* and *body, essence* and *existence*), he starts from the concepts of *Concern* (*Sorge*) and *Dread* (*Angst*). *Concern* constitutes the structure of consciousness and is propounded as the ultimate, as having a wholly unique horizon of being. *Dread,* on the other hand (the feeling of

80

being on the verge of nothingness) constitutes man's daily conscious existence (his existential condition). *Concern* is the essence of *Dread,* while *Dread* is existence. It is when man can get out of the existential bonds of *Dread* and can comprehend *Concern* as its essence, that he begins to live in full consciousness and with true knowledge of himself. By elevating the concept of Concern to the basis of all being, Heidegger posited something universally human as the fundamental principle of the world. Main works: *Sein und Zeit (Being and Time)* (1927); *What is Metaphysics?* (1929).

**Helvétius, Claude Adrien** (1715-1771). French philosopher, born in Paris, who employed the *sensationalism* of CONDILLAC to develop his own form of *materialism.* His theory of *egoism* and *self-interest* as the sole motives of human action were condemned in his time but were later admired by BENTHAM and the English utilitarians. The ultimate ethical ramification of his doctrine was *circumstantialism* (i.e. we are all alike mentally at birth, but circumstances determine our development). Key work: *Essay on the Love of Study* (1737).

**Heraclides** (388-315 B. C.). Greek philosopher, born at Pontus in Asia Minor, he was a disciple of PLATO but specialized mainly in cosmological observations. He discovered that Venus and Mercury revolve around the sun, and was the first thinker in history to advance the view that the earth rotates on its axis once in every twenty-four hours.

**Heraclitus** (c. 536-470 B. C.). Born in Ephesus, he was one of the most vigorous thinkers of Greek antiquity. He opposed the *Milesian school* (which explained the manifold processes of the universe as emanating from a single principle or "world-stuff" called the *infinite*) and held that all things, and the universe as a whole, are in constant, ceaseless flux. *Change* is the only reality — all else is merely a continuous process of passing away. On the basis of this doctrine, he described the world as a kind of *eternal fire;* a consuming movement

81

in which only the orderliness of the succession of things remains the same.

**Herbart, Johann Friedrich** (1776-1841). A pioneer in early psychological research and education, this German thinker, born at Oldenburg, succeeded KANT as professor of philosophy at Königsberg. To him, philosophy was reflection upon the conceptions that are commonly used in experience, and its most important function is to identify and describe those things in objective reality (experience) that correspond to the abstractions of speculation (e.g. substance, causality, etc.). While German idealism proceeded from the individual *knower* (the subject) to the metaphysical problems of nature and the mind, Herbart regarded the *knower* as the highest metaphysical problem. Because the *knower* is the changing product of ideas, the problem is best explored, he felt, by psychological research. Instead of deducing everything from a single, all-embracing principle, he adhered to the principle of *identity* (the axiom that *everything is what it is*). Hence, nothing can be ultimately real if two true, yet contradictory, statements can be made about it; for instance, to say that an object is both one and numerous is to state a contradiction; thus, that object cannot be ultimately real because ultimate reality must be absolutely unitary and without change. Herbart identified psychology with philosophy and attempted to explain ideas in a mathematical and physical way. To him, reality was made up of *reals* (the *uncontradictory things* that constitute reality); ideas arise originally from the collision of reals. Ideas are forces operating in nature much like the electrons of modern physics — they whirl around, so to speak, collide and split, forming new ideas. It is in this process that knowledge is formed. Key works: *Main Points of Logic* (1808); *Main Points of Metaphysics* (1808); *German Metaphysics* (1829).

**Herder, Johann Gottfried** (1744-1803). Born at Möhrungen, Germany, he studied under KANT and went on to become the founder of modern *religious humanism*. He arrived at this humanism through his theories on history. He claimed that man is constituted of a *double essence* — a determined, restricted nature and a free reason. It is his reason that enables man to see his nature as it is reflected in history. But it is his nature that makes the history; and this history shows that man's nature is basically *good*. Why? Because the history of man is basically a history of humanitarianism. Finally, since man's nature is a manifestation of God, the humanitarian streak that shows throughout history is an expression of God's will. Key work: *Ideas on the Philosophy of History of Humanity* (1784-91).

**Hermes, Georg** (1775-1831). German philosopher born at Dreyerwalde, he wrote several books in which he attempted to reconcile the *rationalism* of KANT with the *dogmatism* of the Catholic Church. His ideas were condemned after his death by the Pope (1835). Key work: *Introduction to Philosophy* (1819).

**Hess, Moses** (1812-1875). German born contemporary and associate of MARX. Although "Moritz" was his birth name, he adopted the name "Moses" to emphasize his adherence to Judaism; and in order to show his contempt for the existing moral standards of his day, he married a prostitute, with whom he lived in happiness until his death. Although early on he collaborated with Marx, he later disagreed with him by conceiving of socialism as a prevalently human ideal rather than the inevitable historical result of economic evolution. Neither was his socialism strictly egalitarian; rather, it was an effort to satisfy the wants of human nature, which idea became his primary standard of judging human institutions. Key works: *European Triarchy* (1841); *German Ideology*, with Karl Marx (1846).

**Hillel of Verona** (1220-1295). Jewish physician and philosopher who lived in Italy. His *theory of the soul* followed partly that of AVERROËS in assuming that a Universal Active Intellect acts upon the soul of the individual and helps it to realize its powers. He rejected, however, the other Averröistic view that immortality consists in the union of the human intellect with the Universal Active Intellect.

**Hobbes, Thomas** (1588-1679). Born at Westport in Malmesbury, this English thinker was at one time tutor to Charles II of France and later secretary to FRANCIS BACON. He professed *materialism,* seeking to explain everything on the basis of mechanistic principles. He rejected most traditional philosophical concepts as useless abstractions. He considered knowledge to be *empirical* (i.e. accruing from observation and experience only) both in origin and results, and regarded the study of bodies and their movements as the only concern of philosophy. He divided philosophy into four sub-sciences: (1) *geometry* (describing the movements of bodies in space); (2) *physics* (describing the effects of moving bodies on one another); (3) *ethics* (describing the movements of the nervous system); (4) *politics* (describing the effects of nervous systems on one another). Thus, his philosophy was devoted to ascertaining the laws of motion. The *first law of motion* appears in every organic body in its very tendency to movement; in man, the *first law of motion* becomes the *first natural right* (the right to self-preservation and self-assertion). This causes all bodies, whether organic or inorganic (men, animals, objects, ideas, etc.) to enter into the primary condition of life — collision and conflict (and war). The *second law of motion* is a kind of recoil from the condition of collision, and impels bodies (and men) to relinquish their natural right to self-assertion for a similar relinquishment on the part of fellow bodies (and men). Out of these two laws of natural motion there necessarily arise, on the human level, such things as social contracts, which are the basis for the state. Key works: *De Corpore*

*(On Bodies,* 1655); *De Homine (On Man,* 1658); *De Cive (On the State);* Leviathan (1651).

**Hocking, William Ernest** (1873- ). A contemporary professor of philosophy at Harvard Univ., he was born at Cleveland. In his social and political thought he has attempted to reconcile the divergent ideas of *laissez-faire capitalism* and *socialistic collectivism* through an emphasis on the inherently worthy goals of the individual acting in conjunction with the inherently worthy goals of government. Key works: *Man and the State* (1926); *Lasting Elements of Individualism* (1937).

**Hodgson, Shadworth** (1832-1912). An ascetic English philosopher who, through his vigorous criticism of the philosophy of KANT, prepared the way for what is known as *new realism.* His method was to analyze the content of consciousness without any preconceived notions about its origins or nature. He rejected Kant's materialistic approach to reality and directed his own philosophy to an investigation of invisible reality (the unseen world). Such investigation should not be motivated by speculative conviction (abstract knowledge), he insisted, but only by moral compulsion. Key work: *The Metaphysics of Experience* (1898).

**Höffding, Harald** (1843-1931). Danish philosopher who taught for many years at the Univ. of Copenhagen, where he was born. He became Denmark's most important modern thinker. He held that the world of reality is unknowable as a whole, although conscious experience and its unity afford the best keys for unlocking the riddle of the universe. In other words, experience is the only path to true knowledge, yet experience is too difficult a problem in itself for philosophers to solve. He wrote significant works on KIERKEGAARD and ROUSSEAU. Key work: *The Concept of Will* (1906).

**Holbach, Paul Henri, Baron d'** (1723-1789). German nobleman who settled in Paris and became a French citizen. A severe and outspoken atheist, he was highly critical of religion and the Church. He developed the doctrine of *eternal change* (nothing in nature is fixed; nature is capable of and is forever giving rise to new organisms, hitherto unknown; man is not exempt from this law of change; man cannot exist without nature, though nature can exist without man). By this doctrine, man has no special role in the universe; all things traditionally postulated about his uniqueness and worth are meaningless. Main work: *The System of Nature* (1770).

**Howison, George Holmes** (1834-1916). American thinker who taught philosophy for many years at the Univ. of California. He opposed all doctrines that held there is only one fundamental reality. He developed instead a doctrine of *personalistic idealism* (which affirms the uniqueness and moral nature of finite individuals) and asserted that consciousness is human and original to man in all respects (and not an earthly manifestation of divine or universal consciousness). Key work: *The Conception of God* (1897).

**Hsün Ch'ing** (c. 298-238 B. C.). Chinese philosopher who was also known as Hsün Tzū, he developed the most purely philosophical strain in Confucianism. Although he adopted some Taoist ideas, he remained faithful to Confucianism. However, he was a severe critic of MENCIUS; while Mencius believed all men are naturally good, Hsün Ch'ing maintained that all men are naturally evil. He saw in labor — "the good of construction" — an antidote to "the evil of destruction" that was natural to the world. Toward this end, he believed firmly in the necessity of moral order and individual self-perfection, while strongly opposing a belief in fate.

**Huizinga, Johan** (1872-1945). Long a professor of philosophy at the Univ. of Leyden in Holland, he developed a philosophy of *culture* in which culture is described as that condition of society which contains a harmonious balance of material and spiritual values, and a harmonious ideal spurring the community's activities to a convergence of all efforts toward the attainment of that ideal. Key work: *Homo Ludens* (1938).

**Humboldt, Wilhelm von** (1767-1835). German thinker whose principal importance was as a philosopher of *language*. He felt language to be the key to the expression of ideas and was astonished that up to his time no real attempt had been made to create a universal language of philosophy. He claimed that language was man's greatest and most vital invention; however, that it was abysmally neglected, especially by philosophy. Ideas mean nothing unless they are articulated, and language is the principal mediator between man and the reality of his ideas and concepts. He held that language is not just a voice or tool, but itself a primary act of man's nature, and should be considered even before such qualities as reason, consciousness, etc., in attempting to comprehend man's nature and its relation to reality. Likewise, language is a universal activity, the same as the life of the spirit and the condition of history. Key work: *The Origin of Grammatical Forms* (1822).

**Hume, David** (1711-1776). Born at Edinburgh, he was an important Scottish thinker who expanded on the conclusions of LOCKE and BERKELEY to develop a determined and thoroughgoing philosophy of *skepticism*. Was a patron of ROUSSEAU during the later's English exile, but later quarrelled bitterly with him. His thought was centered in an analysis of the mind, which, he claimed, consisted of nothing but a *series of sensations* (or ideas). From this he concluded that the cause and effect relation evident in the world was only *apparent* and not certifiable, because sensations (ideas) were, as a matter of habit, joined or compared in the mind.

Since knowledge results solely from the comparison of sensations (ideas), it consists merely of the intrinsic *resem-
blances* between such sensations (ideas). And because *re-
semblance* consists of nothing more than sensations (ideas)
that resemble one another, there are no abstract, general
ideas. In this way, he doubted the possibility that knowledge
could be certain. He carried this skepticism into ethics, as
well. Since there are no logically compelling arguments for
moral and religious propositions, the principles of morality
and religion must be explained as deriving naturally rather
than supernaturally; furthermore, they must be described
in terms of human mental habits and social customs. Hence,
to replace the absence of ultimate knowledge or values,
Hume offered an adherence to common sense and in a faith
in the good possibilities of man. Key works: *A Treatise
on Human Nature* (1737-39); *Enquiry Concerning Morals;
Enquiry Concerning Human Understanding.*

**Husserl, Edmund** (1859-1938). German thinker born at Prossnitz
and sometimes referred to as the father of modern *existentialism,* he studied under BRENTANO at the Univ. of Vienna
and later taught at the Universities of Halle, Göttingen and
Freiburg. Of Jewish origin, he fell victim to the Nazi academic purge. He developed the philosophy of *phenomenology*
(the study of the relationship of the conscious mind to objects), later refined by HEIDEGGER, one of his students. He
claimed that the correct procedure for any philosophy must
be the understanding of things as they are presented in the
form of empirical evidence to experience, and that such understanding must be *intuitive.* Key work: *Investigations in
Logic* (1900).

**Hutcheson, Francis** (1694-1747). Scottish moral philosopher; born
at Drumalig, educated at Glasgow, he died in Dublin. He propounded the doctrine of *moral sense* (i.e. all activity is based
on the compulsions of an *inborn conscience*) and originated

the phrase "the greatest happiness for the greatest number" which later, in the hands of BENTHAM, became the motto of utilitarianism. Key work: *Inquiry into the Origin of Our Ideas of Beauty and Virtue* (1725).

**Hypatia** (c. 360-415). Egyptian mathematician and philosopher, she was born at Alexandria. She was a follower of PLOTINUS and advocated the fundamental doctrines of *neo-platonism* (especially, that our minds can transcend our practical experience and enter into mystical knowledge of the true nature of things).

# I

**Ibn Gabirol, Solomon.** See AVICEBRON.

**Ibn Khaldun** (1332-1406). Born at Tunis in North Africa, this Islamic philosopher was the first to establish history ·as a science. He regarded the body of mankind, like the body of the individual man, as a living and growing organism, and tried to find its cause and purpose by identifying it with the causes and purposes of history. Key work: *Preface to History.*

**Ibn Roshd, Mohammad.** See AVERROËS.

**Inge, William Ralph** (1860-1954). English theologian and philosopher, he was born at Crayke, died at Wellingford, and was for many years (1911-34) the Dean of St. Paul's Cathedral in London. He claimed that the similarities between PLATO's *idealism* and Christian *mysticism* were so great that, for him, there was no difference or disparity between philosophy and religion. He viewed the world as a combination of material *object* and mental (spiritual) *idea,* and declared that ultimate reality consists of the union of the *material* and the *ideal* (spiritual) in the harmony of love. Such, he said, was precisely the contribution to the history of wisdom made by Christ. Key works: *Faith and Knowledge* (1904); *Speculations on the Soul* (1911).

**Ipuwer** (c. 2500 B. C.). One of the earliest of the ancient Egyptian thinkers and the world's first social philosopher, he was an intense and thoroughgoing *pessimist*. He felt that the *will to live* was the source of all evil and recommended race suicide as a means of terminating human misery.

**Isvarakrsna** (c. 200-300 A. D.). A thinker usually connected with the philosophy of *sankhya,* probably the oldest of the six traditional systems of Indian philosophy. *Sankhya* shares with other systems a belief in gods, demi-gods and demons, but considers them mortal and subject to the Indian theological law of transmigration. However, it denies the existence of a universal God. It is basically a *pessimistic* philosophy, regarding all existence as suffering. It is also *dualistic,* insisting on the fundamental difference between *soul* and *matter.* Salvation from suffering is achieved by grasping the absolute difference between the soul and everything material.

# J

**Jacobi, Friedrich Heinrich** (1743-1818). Born at Düsseldorf, he was a German opponent of KANT. He proposed a philosophy of *feeling* in which he rejected all rationalistic philosophies as incapable of grasping ultimate *reality* because their insights were basically synthetic and manufactured. He propounded instead a system of thought, based on feelings, which claimed to be able to discover truth as it is immediately revealed in consciousness. Key work: *Demonstration of God's Existence* (1763).

**Jamblicus** (c. 270-330). Syrian thinker highly influenced by PLATO. He wrote extensive commentaries on Greek and Oriental theology and transformed the teachings of PLOTINUS into a dogmatic theology of *pantheism.*

**James, William** (1842-1910). Born in New York City, he was one of the most important and influential of American thinkers. After receiving a medical degree at Harvard Univ. (1870), he turned to philosophy and psychology and began a teaching career at Harvard that lasted many years. His main contribution to philosophy came through his *Principles of Psychology* (1890). He espoused a doctrine of *radical empiricism* (which emphasizes the value and examination of immediate concrete experience as a way to truth), which he placed in revolt against the intellectual idealism that reigned in his day. He maintained that experience consists of a *plurality,* or multiplicity, of reality (real units), and that this fact disqualified the possibility of a single, fundamental reality. He not only, like HUME, doubted consciousness, he denied it. He insisted that reality was nothing but the stream of objective experiences, and he rejected the notion that knowledge could consist of the relation between consciousness and the objects in the world of which it is conscious. Key works: *Varieties of Religious Experience* (1902); *Pragmatism* (1907); *Essays in Radical Empiricism* (1912).

**Jaspers, Karl** (1883-   ). Born at Oldenburg, Germany, he began his career as a psychiatrist, but turned to philosophy and became one of modern Germany's foremost thinkers. His thought begins with a concern with the mind of the philosopher in relation to his philosophy. He claimed that the distinguishing trait of the philosophical mind is *personal faith.* Such faith transcends objective knowledge and is grounded in reason. Thus, empirical knowledge is of minor importance; it is the knowledge derived from rational insights that counts towards truth. A *theist,* he criticizes Christianity and Judaism for claiming absolute truth and insists that the aim of philosophical inquiry is to recognize the uniqueness of man as an individual and to help man attain independence. To him, independence is the same as achieving transcendence — that awareness of truth which is identical with certainty of God. Jaspers has had much influence on the development of modern existentialism. Key works: *The Spiritual Situation of Time* (1931); *Reason and Existence* (1935); *Philosophy of Existence* (1938).

**Jeans, James** (1877-1946). English astronomer whose scientific discoveries about the cosmos prompted him to turn to philosophy as a means of their expression. He subscribed to PLATO's utterance that "God is a mathematician." Yet the physical world, said Jeans, is not the highest reality of God's creation. "The universe begins to look more and more like

94

a great thought than a great machine," he once wrote. He pictured reality "as a deep-flowing stream; the world of appearance is its surface, below which we cannot see." However, by constantly probing into its depths, science is now and then capable of catching a clue to its mystery. What science shows us is this: the world of appearance and the world of reality are but different aspects of the same truth — that all existence is a *mathematical pattern* which puts everything in its proper place and its proper time. Key work: *Through Space and Time* (1934).

**Jevons, William Stanley** (1835-1882). English philosopher and teacher, he was born at Liverpool. Logic was his main concern. His most singular contribution to philosophy was contained in his key work, *Principles of Science* (1874), in which he elaborated a theory of logic based on inductive reasoning. Motivated in part by his disagreement with MILL's conception of induction as depending on a process of elimination, Jevons formulated his own doctrine of inductive reasoning in which hypotheses, framed by the informal insight of the scientist, are subsequently confirmed by evaluating the evidence in their favor in accordance with the *calculus of probability*. At best, and by this method, inductive conclusions are just barely certain, as against MILL's declaration of their capability of complete certainty.

**Joad, Cyril E. M.** (1891-1953). Distinguished contemporary British thinker who began his career in philosophy as an intense *realist* unalterably opposed to idealism. However, he later became a staunch defender of religion against materialistic critics. He asserted that it was fallacy to assume, as he claimed materialists did, that to expose the origins of a thing is tantamount to describing its present nature. Materialists criticized religious beliefs and dogmas on the basis of the fact that they were inventions of man, not existing realities or truths. But, according to Joad, to show how a belief arises does not constitute a description of it, much less its refutation. Key work: *Guide to the Philosophy of Morals and Politics* (1938).

**Jodl, Friedrich** (1848-1914). Austrian ethical philosopher who devoted himself to developing a humanistic and naturalistic ethics (i.e. devoid of any religious compulsions). He also outlined a new kind of religion based on ethical and national culture. Key work: *History of Ethics as a Philosophical Science* (1882-89).

**John of Salisbury** (c. 1115-1180). Medieval critic of Scholasticism, he advocated reforms in logic. He was among the earliest adherents of the strict separation between Church and state. He had a practical attitude toward knowledge: he rejected what was useless and contrary to good life, and accepted what was favorable to the good, even though positive logical proof might not be found to support the latter. In this respect he anticipated the much later *instrumentalism* of DEWEY and others. Key work: *Beyond Logic.*

**Jouffroy, Theodore Simon** (1796-1842). French philosopher, he was born at Pontets and died in Paris. He was preoccupied with the idea of human destiny, a preoccupation motivated by his loss of faith in Christianity. He felt that religious dogma failed to deal satisfactorily with the fundamental question of man's final end; that man's anguish about his destiny was only heightened by theological obscurantism. Hence, he claimed that philosophy, which at least addressed itself rationally to this problem, should replace religion.

**Justin Martyr** (c. 110-165). The earliest defense of Christianity using philosophical arguments was made by Justin, who later suffered a martyr's death in Rome. He especially tried to convert pagan philosophers to his creed by using their own terms. He was born at Flavia Neapolis, formerly Shechem, in Samaria. Key work: *Apologies.*

# K

**Kallen, Horace Meyer** (1882-    ). American thinker who originally came from Berenstadt, Germany. He has taught philosophy at Harvard and Wisconsin Universities, and has written many popular books on life in America. His central philosophical views revolve around his doctrine that the world was not created for the pleasure of man; rather, man was created for the purpose of improving the world. Key works: *Art and Freedom* (1942); *The Liberal Spirit* (1948).

**Kant, Immanuel** (1724-1804). One of the world's most important philosophers, he was born and died at Königsberg, Germany. Became tutor to the family of Count Keyserling (1755) and was appointed professor of logic and metaphysics at the Univ. of Königsberg (1770). Trained in the philosophy of LEIBNIZ, he was influenced by the mathematical theories of ISAAC NEWTON, by the psychological theories of LOCKE, and especially by the philosophy of HUME. His own system was rooted in a rationalistic outlook, but sought to implant a comprehensive method and doctrine of experience that would improve upon mere intellectual idealism. His philosophy came to be known as *transcendental idealism* (i.e. knowledge can only be a synthetic and relative product of logical consciousness). He began by questioning the assumption, common to dogmatic metaphysics, that knowledge can be apprehended through concepts. His question was: "By what right and within what limits may reason make syn-

97

thetic judgments about sense experience, judgments that are synthetic and independent of the sense experience itself?" His answer, on the theoretical plane, was that the function of reason is to relate, or synthesize, the data of sense. In making any synthesis, the mind must rely upon the validity of certain basic principles (e.g. causality) that cannot be proven from sense experience yet are indispensable to any study of experience as a connected and unified whole. If these basic principles cannot be derived from sense data, then they must be *a priori* (existing logically *before* the materials to which they relate). That these principles exist cannot be doubted, since, although they cannot be proved as coming from sense experience, they are verifiable by experience. He called such principles *"transcendentals"* (i.e. while they are undoubtedly *in* experience, they transcend or are distinct in *source* from sense materials). For instance, space and time are *empirically real* because they are actually present in experience and can be perceived there; by the same token, they are *transcendentally ideal,* since they are ideas that the mind imposes on the data of sense. From this basic conception, Kant developed *synthetic, a priori principles* for all the branches of philosophy. In logic, he termed them *categories;* there are twelve categories, three each pertaining to *quality, quantity, relation* and *modality.* He showed that without these categories (*synthetic, a priori principles*), there could be no knowledge or experience. In other words, in order to know something, one must proceed from something *prior* in knowledge, already known. The *categories* themselves are the first things known, through reasoned deductions from experience, and therefore are the *first principles* of knowledge — it is imperative that they be known before the mind attempts to know other things. To put it another way, sense experience itself is inarticulate, and knowledge of it requires something articulate from which, or by which, to make an articulated conclusion; thus, the necessity for *a priori, synthetic principles* that serve as the starting points for all investigations. However, Kant maintained that these principles, or *categories,* cannot be used beyond experience to define such things as metaphysical entities (e.g. God, soul, etc.). If the principles are valid *in* experience precisely because they are the necessary conditions *of* experience, there is no way of judging their applicability to objects beyond experience. Thus, he denied the possibility of a science of metaphysics. Nevertheless, he was able to assert that although we are not capable of knowing *things-in-themselves,* we can know things as *phenomena;* indeed, for the sake of morality and human affairs we need such metaphysical entities (transcendental concepts) as God, soul, freedom, immortality, etc. Toward this end, he posited, again *a priori,* the category of man's freedom — the principle that the will of man is free and autonomous. This is a category unto itself, a law of nature. The *categorical imperative* deriving from this law is that man must act on maxims that can be identified with the universal laws of nature, because reason, through *a priori* categories, gives nature its laws. Main works: *Critique of Pure Reason* (1781-1787); *Critique of Practical Reason* (1788); *Critique of Judgment* (1789-1793).

**Kapila** (c. 600 B. C.). A legendary figure of Indian philosophy, he was the founder of the *dualistic-rationalistic* philosophy of *Sankhya* (of which the main doctrine is: whatever changes cannot be conscious and whatever is conscious cannot change; thus, there is a *dual mode of reality* — that which changes and that which does not). Kapila saw the entire world as a living material cycle moving from evolution to dissolution and back again to evolution; he also saw the world as spiritual — i.e. he admitted the existence of a Universal Soul animating all material nature.

**Kierkegaard, Sören** (1813-1855). Danish religious thinker and philosopher whose influence, until a few decades ago, was

99

limited to the Nordic countries. He is now considered by many to be the spiritual father of modern *existentialism;* in the less abstract senses of this movement the appellation is indeed justified, since he was a severely pessimistic social thinker. He held that *eternity* is more important than time; that *sin is* worse than suffering; that man is an egotist and must *experience despair* in order to gain humility; that God is *beyond* man's reason; that Christianity, as desirable as it is in theory, stands opposed to the world, to time, and to reason; and that the interminable paradoxes of life are the inevitable result of man's reflections. He was against orthodox religions and official systematized philosophies (especially the *dialectic* of HEGEL). His own philosophy was aimed at creating difficulties, rather than solving them, since he felt that man became enlightened only through humility, and humility could only be truly got through conflict. He died destitute and, some claim, insane. Key works: *Sickness Unto Death* (1848); *The Diary* (1834-55); *Either/Or* (1843); *Stages on Life's Way* (1845).

**Koffka, Kurt** (1886-1941). With KÖHLER and WERTHEIMER, one of the founders of *Gestalt Psychology.* He emphasized the role of insight in the learning process, in opposition to the conventional emphasis on trial and error. Key work: *The Principles of Gestalt Psychology* (1935).

**Köhler, Wolfgang** (1887- ). An associate of WERTHEIMER and KOFFKA at the Univ. of Frankfort in Germany, he was, with them, the founder of *Gestalt Psychology* (a reaction to the psychic approach in psychology that treats the parts of the psyche; *Gestalt* deals with the whole, claiming that the parts do not exist prior to the whole but derive their existence and character from the whole itself; therefore, the whole should be the prime object of psychology). He later taught psychology at the Univ. of Berlin, then at Swarthmore College in the U. S. Main work: *Gestalt Psychology* (1929).

**Korn, Alejandro** (1860-1936). Was born at San Vicente, Argentina, and died at Buenos Aires. A psychiatrist and physician, he also taught philosophy (1906-30) at the Universities of Buenos Aires and La Plata. He developed a uniquely Argentinian philosophical tradition based on what he considered to be the useful elements of *positivism*. He held that *intuition* was the basis of all knowledge and that all concepts are expressions of immediate evidence and not conclusions of reasoning. Key works: *The Concept of Science* (1926); *Philosophical Observations* (1935).

**Krause, Karl Christian** (1781-1832). A younger contemporary of KANT who tried to formulate a reconciliation between the divergent principles of *theism* and *pantheism,* which he called *panentheism*. Key work: *Lectures on the System of Philosophy* (1828).

**Kropotkin, Peter Alekseievitch** (1842-1921). Born into nobility at Moscow, he became a political philosopher famous for his doctrine of *anarchism*. Like BAKUNIN's, his anarchism was not a doctrine of violence, but an outline for peace. He advanced a theory of *mutual aid* as a rationale for eliminating all forms of government except true self-government. He based this theory on the evidence of various studies of animal behavior, and his main source for inspiration was DARWIN's *theory of evolution through the survival of the fittest*. Kropotkin insisted that *mutual aid* is as important a principle of nature as *mutual hate;* that *mutual hate,* and the struggle for existence, as Darwin had shown, exists only with respect to different species; that among the same species there is a spirit of mutual *cooperation* for existence; and that since man is a single species, all men should cooperate and help each other to survive. Thus, "the aspirations of man are at one with nature," and "mutual aid, therefore, is the predominant fact of nature. . . ." Key works: *Memoirs of a Revolutionist* (1901); *Mutual Aid* (1904).

**Külpe, Oswald** (1862-1915). Opposed to the *idealism* of KANT, he was the foremost pioneer of *realism* in Germany. He advocated the theory of *realization* (which considered the findings of science to be the discovery of universal realities). This theory was centered in his belief that the universals of things are as real in the abstract as the things themselves are in existence. Key work: *Theory of Knowledge and Natural Science* (1910).

# L

**Lachelier, Jules** (1832-1918). French, he taught for many years at the École Normale Superieure in Paris and had considerable influence on such of his students as BOUTROUX and BERGSON. His own philosophy was modelled on the *idealism* of KANT, with overtones of French *spiritualism*. Main work: *Psychology and Metaphysics* (1885).

**Laird, John** (1887-1946). Born at Durris, England, he was an exponent of British *new realism* (the mind is simply an integral part of nature and has no unique character or status). He claimed that knowledge, as well as value, cannot be subjective but must be derived from the objects of the universe. Key work: *A Study in Realism* (1920).

**Lalande, André** (1867-  ). Born at Dijon, France, he is the author of the *Technical and Critical Vocabulary of Philosophy,* which has contributed greatly to standardizing the semantics of philosophy. His own thought is based on the notion of two antagonistic laws of the universe (*evolution* and *involution*). Life and its processes result from a compromise between the two tendencies, the first of which directs itself to increasing individual differences, the second to eliminating them. Man's *will* must choose between the two. Key work: *Evolutionist Illusions* (1931).

**Lambert, Johann Heinrich** (1728-1777). German thinker strongly influenced by LEIBNIZ and WOLFF. He attempted a reconciliation between *rationalism* (knowledge derived from thought) and *empiricism* (knowledge derived from experience), and laid the foundations for the critical philosophy of KANT.

**La Mettrie, Julien Offray de** (1709-1751). Born at St. Malo, he was a French philosopher of *materialism* (i.e. matter is the source of all things) who held that the soul is a product of the body and that the brain has "thought muscles" which enable it to think (just as the leg has "walk muscles"). Key works: *The Natural History of the Soul* (1745); *The Man-Machine* (1747).

**Lange, Friedrich Albert** (1828-1875). German thinker, celebrated for his *History of Materialism* (1866) which, although it demonstrated the limitations of *materialistic* thought in metaphysics, also showed the value of materialistic views as a stimulus to critical thought. Other key work: *The Fundamentals of Mathematical Psychology* (1864).

**Lao-Tze** (c. 604-560 B. C.). Legendary Chinese philosopher, by many considered to be the founder of Taoism (tao chia). He was a native of what is now Honan Province in Southern China. Little is known about his life except that he was probably a priest-teacher and that he was an acquaintance of CONFUCIUS. By advocating a doctrine of *inaction,* he worked to preserve the declining culture of Yin, his suppressed people; whereas Confucius worked to promote the culture of Chou, the ruling people. In Taoism, he propounded a doctrine of *reality* that is different from a notion of the world perceptible by the senses — it is a cosmic order of nature that cannot be grasped by human intellect or expressed in words. In many regards it is similar to the Idea reality assumed by PLATO, and even more so to the Hindu distinction between the world of appearance and true existence. Key work: *The Celestial Laws.*

**Lassalle, Ferdinand** (1825-1864). German philosopher, born at Breslau. As founder of the social democratic movement in Germany, he opposed MARX' ideas for a worldwide socialism and worked for an enlightened, progressive and peaceful Germany through rational nationalism. Metaphysically, he largely subscribed to the doctrines of HERACLITUS. Key work: *The Philosophy of Heraclitus* (1860).

**Lavelle, Louis** (1883-1931). A student of HANNEQUIN at the Univ. of Lyons in France, he later taught philosophy at the College of France and developed the doctrine of *spiritual existentialism* (i.e. man, fluctuating as he does between notions of God and notions of no-God, exists in alternating periods of joy and sorrow; as an antidote to this, man has developed a quality of *creative nostalgia* which enables his soul to transcend joy and sorrow and their existential consequences — his soul thus rises to a level of spiritual communion with the Absolute). Lavelle's metaphysics expands upon this doctrine: he held that metaphysical speculation addresses itself to *experience,* but to a special kind of experience — a *self-generated experience* that lifts man above the egoistic world and places his consciousness in direct relation to truth. His notion of *experience* was similar to BERGSON's notion of *intuition* (in that they both possess creative qualities); however, while Bergson's intuition relates to *duration,* Lavelle's intuition (experience) relates to *eternity;* while to Bergson intuition is contraposed to reason, to Lavelle, reason necessarily prolongs the work of intuition (experience). Key works: *The "I" and Its Destiny* (1926); *The Act* (1927).

**Leibniz, Gottfried Wilhelm von** (1646-1716). Born at Leipzig, Germany, and educated at the Universities of Jena and Altdorf, he was trained in law, diplomacy, history, mathematics, theology and philosophy, and became the most notable thinker of 17th century Germany. His philosophy was based on a conception of the universe that united beauty with mathematical order and saw a connection between naturalistic facts and metaphysical ideas, or feelings. He described the vital elements of this world as *monads* (true atoms that exist metaphysically); their co-existence and relations are regulated by a pre-established harmony, which is the work of God. Leibniz devoted much of his work to the reform of science, a reform he felt could be effected by the use of a universal scientific language and a calculus of reasoning. Toward this end he invented and developed a language of symbols in which complex concepts could be expressed by combinations of symbols representing simple concepts. In this way, almost all concepts could be defined. His method was a forerunner of modern symbolic logic. Key works: *Discourse on Metaphysics* (1686); *New System of Nature* (1695).

**Leone Ebreo.** See ABRAVANEL, JUDAH.

**Lequier, Jules** (1814-1862). French philosopher, he was born at Quentin and died at Rosaire. He left no formal written works, but fragments of his writings had an enormous influence on RENOUVIER and other 19th century French philosophers. The problem of *freedom* seemed to have been his main preoccupation. He rejected all determinist and evolutionist doctrines and claimed that freedom is the one condition required for fruitful thought. He eventually identified freedom with knowledge itself.

**Lessing, Gotthold Ephraim** (1729-1781). German poet, dramatist and critic, he was born in Saxony and died in Brunswick. He was a champion of religious tolerance whose best remembered work, the drama *Nathan the Wise* (1779), was written as an attempt to encourage liberation from strict religious creed and the prejudices and destructive passions deriving therefrom. The touchstone of his thought was that the striving for truth is more important and beneficial to man than the possession of truth. He held that there are two kinds of religion: a universal natural religion to which all men are beholden by virtue of the fact that the religious impulse is a part of man's nature; and particular revealed religions which express some divine idea. The best revealed religion is that which displays the least number of disagreements with the universal natural religion.

**Leucippus** (c. 490-430 B. C.). Born in Abdera, he was a contemporary of EMPEDOCLES and ANAXAGORAS, and founder of the *Abderan* school of ancient Greek philosophy. He was also founder of the doctrine of *atomism* (i.e. atoms are the primary substances of the universe), and developed the principle that all differences in the quality of things in nature can be reduced to differences in quantity. Thus, there is no unity of Being (which was the view of PARMENIDES); rather, there are as many *beings* as there are things. He described these multiple *beings* as existing in an *infinity of identical atoms*. These atoms are separated and distinguished from one another by Non-Being (empty space). Things come into existence by virtue of the motion of these atoms in space and their accidental coming together.

**Lévy-Bruhl, Lucien** (1857-1939). Born at Paris, he was a distinguished professor of philosophy at the Sorbonne (1899-1939). His work represents a sociological and anthropological approach to philosophy. Through his studies of primitive, pre-rational man, he discovered that such man perceived the external world differently than does modern, rational man. Key work: *The Primitive Mentality* (1922).

**Lewes, George Henry** (1817-1878). Born in London, he was a man of letters and a gifted, versatile, though untrained, philosopher. Inspired by the positivism of COMTE, he attempted to remove from philosophy all the metaphysical elements that he considered insoluble and meaningless, and sought to reduce everything in philosophy to terms of *ex-*

*perience.* He opposed the *mechanistic* theories of organic processes and introduced the theory of *emergence* in explanation of how things come into being. Key work: *Comte's Philosophy of the Sciences* (1853); *Problems of Life and Mind* (1874-79).

**Lewis, Clarence Irving** (1883-1947). Born at Stoneham, Massachusetts, he was an eminent professor of philosophy at Harvard. He specialized in the study of logic and in the advancement of a *naturalistic ethics.* As a result of his work in logic he concluded that there is a plurality of logical truth. He declared ethics to be an empirical science and insisted that ethical questions must be reduced to those of natural sciences, to be tested and solved purely on the basis of the findings of those sciences. Key works: *Symbolic Logic,* with C. H. Langford (1932); *An Analysis of Knowledge and Valuation* (1947).

**Lichtenberg, Georg Christoph** (1742-1799). A German skeptical philosopher who arranged his thought into aphorisms that gained much popularity in his time.

**Lipps, Theodor** (1851-1914). A German psychologist and philosopher born at Walhalben. He is important for his development of the theory of *empathy* (every artistic object represents a living being; *empathy* is the psychic state we experience when we project ourselves into the life of such objects, and is what enables us to relate to them). He posited empathy as the source of knowledge about other egos and taught that philosophy ought to be a science of inner experience coordinated with natural science — in other words, that it should be virtually identical with psychology. Key work: *Aesthetics* (1903-06).

**Locke, John** (1632-1704). English, he was born at Wrington and died at Oates. He was educated at Oxford. The first great

British empirical philosopher, he developed a whole political philosophy based on *empiricism*. He began by denying the existence of eternal categories, principles or ideas from which, allegedly, all our thought is derived. He claimed instead that our knowledge is obtained purely from sense experience and is refined by reflection upon the things that affect the senses. Even seemingly abstract concepts (universals such as substance, cause and effect, etc.) have their causes directly from reflection upon experience — man merely intuits these things. Which is not to say that real knowledge of these universal ideas does not exist; rather, *it does not exist for man*. Thus, man's knowledge is limited, and he must function exclusively within the limits of his senses. Locke employed this doctrine in formulating his long-lived political and economic views. He rejected the notion of the divine right of kings, as well as the authority of the Bible and the Church in temporal affairs. He maintained that political sovereignty rests upon the consent of the governed. His political philosophy is strongly felt in the American Constitution and Declaration of Independence. Key works: *Two Treatises on Government* (1689); *An Essay on Human Understanding* (1690).

**Lotze, Rudolph Hermann** (1817-1881). Born at Bautzen, Germany, he was a psychologist and philosopher whose doctrine of *personal idealism* was strongly tempered by a scientific outlook. He felt that the function of science is to demonstrate the coherence in nature; that being is comprised of the relation between substances; that in these relations there is unity; and that this unity is God. Thus, there is an intelligent purpose in the creation and the order of the universe. He further believed that God is good and is personal (in other words, although God is one, he is in the relation of all things, including that of humans); that personality is the highest value; and that the highest value is that which is most real. Finally, he believed that the unity of law, matter and force, and all other aspects of being, is what produces beauty. Key work: *Metaphysics* (1879).

**Lovejoy, Arthur Oncken** (1873-1962). An American philosopher born in Berlin, he has developed a philosophy which he calls *temporalized realism* (i.e. the most indubitable fact of all our experience is that experience itself is temporal and has no reality outside time). This doctrine has been used by him as a touchstone to be applied to all theories about the nature of reality or of knowledge; he has used it for the rejection of all forms of idealism and monism. To him, since the only reality we can know is our experience, and since we can only know this experience through experience, our notions of reality are confused and totally unverifiable. Key work: *The Great Chain of Being* (1936).

**Lucretius, Titus Carus** (c. 95-55 B. C.). Roman poet-philosopher who, in his well known *On The Nature of Things,* clarified the *atomic theory* of DEMOCRITUS as well as the frequently misinterpreted *pleasure* principles of EPICURUS.

**Lully, Raymond** (1235-1315). Born at Palma on the Spanish island of Majorca, he was often called "Doctor Illuminatus" because of his great learning. His principal philosophical concern was with attempting to reconcile the seeming contraries of life, such as art and science, rationalism and mysticism, abstract philosophy and practical life. Key work: *Ars Generalis* (1275).

**Lu Wang** (1139-1192). Born Lu Hsiang-Shan in China, he imbued Confucianism with the spirit of Buddhism. He considered *mind* to be the embodiment of *reason* and taught that the mind is best developed through tranquil repose, in which state the essences of truth and goodness will be perceived by intuition, and the individual will be united with the universe. Later Confucian philosophies condemned this metaphysical outlook because it regards moral conduct as a mere consequence of an intuitive insight into reality, rather than an end in itself.

# M

**McCosh, James** (1811-1894). Scottish philosopher who was born at Carskeoch. He taught logic and metaphysics at Queen's College, Belfast (1851-68) and was the president of Princeton College in Scotland. His central thesis was that there exist in the human mind certain constituent principles that determine the forms of the mind's experience and guarantee the objectivity of its fundamental opinions. These principles are *intuitions,* and since they determine the forms of experience they cannot be repudiated by the evidences of experience, even though these evidences may be contrary to the forms. Based on this, McCosh sought to reconcile religion with evolutionary theories. He declared that the age-old notion of the divinity of the world's origin is *intuitive* (i.e. formed by constituent principles of the mind), thus true. Hence, evolutionary theories are valid only if they are accepted not as negating religious notions of the divine origin of the world but as accentuating and glorifying the mystery of creation as confirmed by intuition. Key work: *The Religious Aspect of Evolution* (1890).

**McDougall, William** (1871-1938). English psychologist, born at Chatterton, who lectured for some years at Oxford before emigrating to the U. S. and accepting professorships at Harvard and Duke Universities. He was an exponent of *purposive psychology* (we are governed by instincts which give us purpose but which cannot be explained). In philosophy, he propounded a *dualistic* doctrine, similar to that of DES-

CARTES, which held that the universe consists of two fundamentally different substances: *mind* and *matter*. Mind is *thinking* substance; matter is *extended* substance. From this he concluded, in line with his purposive psychology, that it is possible that the soul directs the activities of the body. Main works: *Introduction to Social Psychology* (1908); *Body and Mind* (1911).

**McTaggart, John Ellis** (1866-1925). Born at Aros, Scotland, he was an influential professor of moral science at Cambridge Univ. (1879-1925) and an authority on HEGEL. His own philosophy was *pluralistic* (i.e. reality has more than one fundamental principle). Key work: *The Nature of Existence* (1821).

**Mach, Ernst** (1838-1916). Physicist and philosopher, he was born at Turas, Germany. He was a professor of physics, first at the Univ. of Prague, then at the Univ. of Vienna. In philosophy, he began as a *sensationalist* (i.e. facts can only be received through the senses and cannot be scientifically proved). Like NEWTON, he held that hypotheses are useless and that the only way to test a scientific theory is through use — if it proves out in practice, it must then be characterized as a *law of nature*. Key work: *Analysis of Sensations* (1886).

**Machiavelli, Niccolo** (1469-1527). Born at Florence, he was an Italian political theorist who, in his famous work *The Prince* (1513), propounded the principle of *ruthless expediency* on the part of political leaders and statesmen. He declared that every act of a ruler or government is permissible — especially in matters of foreign affairs — as long as those acts work to the advantage of the ruler or government. This work, although the one he is most remembered for, is not consistent with his more considered and longer *Discourses on Livy, Art of War,* or *History of Florence*. He had been a high civil servant and diplomat in the republican government of Florence that came into power with the fall of Savonarola in 1498 and in turn fell to the Medici in 1512. He suffered imprisonment, torture and forced retirement, in the first few months of which, in a blaze of revulsion, he wrote *The Prince*. If it was intended as a serious work, it must be taken as supplementary to his other writings — its precepts applicable in times of crisis or in desperate circumstances that are comparatively rare; if not serious, then as satire, and its dedication to the Medici as ironical. Much of what he says in *The Prince* is a sardonic description of the political practices of his own day and not a recommendation of such practices — Machiavelli, in his own practice as a diplomat and minister, was hardly "Machiavellian." His greatest importance is that he was a founder of a modern school of political science, emphasizing power and how it is held, not what should be done to fulfill a providential scheme.

**Madhva** (c. 1199-1275). The leading *dualistic* philosopher of his time in India. He held that the world and the highest reality are completely different entities; that they are dissimilar in their essence, and therefore non-commutable, non-interchangeable, and without any relation. Key work: *Commentary on the Brahma Sūtra.*

**Maimon, Salomon** (1754-1800). German-Jewish thinker born in Lithuania, and a contemporary and critic of KANT. He wrote historical works in philosophy; tried to expound a system of symbolic logic; and developed a form of *monism* (i.e. there is but one fundamental reality) that influenced many metaphysical thinkers of the post-Kantian period. Key work: *Test of Transcendental Philosophy* (1790).

**Maimonides** (1135-1204). Born in Cordova, Spain, as Moses ben Maimon, he went on to become the leading Jewish philosopher and Talmudic commentator of the Middle Ages. Expelled from Spain at the age of 13, he wandered with his family through various Mediterranean countries. He finally

113

went to Palestine (1165) and ultimately settled in Fostat, Egypt, where he made his living as a physician and died. His *Guide To The Perplexed* contains the summa of Jewish philosophical thought up to his time. Shaped — as was the thought of most Middle Age thinkers — by ARISTOTLE, his philosophy was devoted to an exposition and criticism of the teachings of the Jewish religion, as well as to problems of God and the world. He exerted great influence on the Catholic scholastic philosophers of the 13th century.

**Maine de Biran, François Pierre** (1766-1824). A French psychological philosopher, he was born at Bergerac. He revolted against the dominant psychologies of his time, materialism and sensationalism, and developed, under the influence of KANT and FICHTE, an *idealistic* and *voluntaristic* psychology in which the mind directly experiences the activity of its will and at the same time experiences the resistance offered to it by what he called the *non-moi*. From this, he interpreted philosophical universals (cause, motion, substance, etc.) as also experienced by the will. Ultimately, then, God was also able to be experienced. Key work: *The Decomposition of Thought* (1805).

**Malebranche, Nicolas** (1638-1715). Born in Paris, he embraced the philosophy of DESCARTES and was principally concerned with the relation between body and mind, as well as with the sources of knowledge. Contrary to Descartes, however, reason to him was not a cause. To him, there was no cause in the world but God. All being, all knowing, all acting, are caused by God. Man has only the faculties of desire and choice, which constitute his freedom. Thus, what man identifies through his reason to be the causes and causal connections of things are not real but are only apparent, or *occasional,* causes. Causality, then, is not valid as a principle of reason, since God is the cause of all things, including knowledge. However, he believed that reason was the way to faith, therefore to God. To him, reason is the intelligent conclusion that comes from the evidence of the senses; this conclusion points to the direct relation between man and God. He believed also that the mind and body cannot possibly interact. Hence, like GEULINCX, he concluded that God enacts bodily movements on the occasion of corresponding mental processes, so that what appears as natural interrelated cause and effect is only God exercising his control over things. Key works: *Investigations of Truth* (1674); *Reflections on Bodily Pre-Motion* (1714).

**Manicheus** (c. 215-276). Born in Persia, his real name was Mani. He became the leader of Manicheanism, a new religion incorporating certain elements of Christianity and ancient Persian beliefs mainly advanced by ZOROASTER. He taught that *virtue* is a principle embodied in the spirit, while *vice* is a principle embodied in matter; and that the world is a battlefield on which the war between virtue (God) and vice (the devil) is waged. AUGUSTINE was a follower of Manicheanism before he converted to Catholicism.

**Marcel, Gabriel** (1889-   ). Important contemporary French philosopher and religious thinker. Born in Paris and raised in a free-thought atmosphere, he eventually converted to Catholicism (1929). He has become the leading exponent of *Christian existentialism* (i.e. that form of Christian thought that addresses itself to a theology embodied in direct spiritual experience rather than to formal, conceptual theology). He holds that man, in his role as a *receptive* being (i.e. receiving things from past experience), becomes a *creative* being by virtue of the fact that his receptivity is active and not passive. Contrary to the conventional existential view that *existence* precedes *essence* (i.e. man is responsible for and the cause of things in the world), he insists that *essence* precedes *existence* (i.e. things are caused outside of man — by God). Existence in itself has no meaning; it receives its meaning from essence. He demonstrates God by analogy — the earth would be an uninhabitable darkness without the presence and power of the light that shines upon it from above; this light is precisely that upon which no greater light can be shed, since it is itself the source of light. Main works: *Being and Having* (1918-33); *The Mystery of Being* (1951).

**Marcus Aurelius.** See AURELIUS.

**Maritain, Jacques** (1882-   ). Born in Paris and educated at the Sorbonne, where he studied under BERGSON. He converted to Catholicism at the age of 24, and much of his thought has since been devoted to the philosophical defense of Catholic dogma. An ardent advocate of the philosophy of AQUINAS, he stresses the applicability of Scholastic philosophy to modern problems. His most significant philosophical view maintains that the value of the human person is rooted in and substantiated by an order that is created by and strives toward God. Main works: *Introduction to Philosophy* (1930); *Seven Lessons on Being* (1934); *The Degrees of Knowledge* (1937).

**Marsiglio** (1270-1342). Italian political philosopher, he was born at Padua. He became a close friend of WILLIAM OF OCKHAM and influenced the latter's political views. Marsiglio held that the legislative power in the state, as well as in the Church, should reside in the majority of the people. He rejected the Church's authority in civil affairs and denied that the pope had the right to exercise secular powers. He was one of the first of the medieval thinkers to advance modern notions of democracy. Key work: *In Defense of Peace* (1324).

**Marx, Karl** (1818-1883). Born at Trier, Germany, of a Jewish family, he died in London. Educated at the Universities of Bonn and Berlin, he received his doctorate from Berlin

116

(1841). He was much influenced by the philosophical method of HEGEL, and used the Hegelian view of history (*dialectic*) to propound his own radical social, political and economic views, which have since become of signal importance in the recent history of the world. He moved to Paris (1844) and became committed to the philosophy of *communism*. He wrote copiously on both abstract and practical matters and composed, with his close friend ENGELS, the *Manifesto of the Communist Party* (1848). He later moved to Brussels, then to London, where he lived until his death. His basic philosophical doctrines, from which his economic and political views derive, have been distorted both by Soviet interpretation and implementation, and by Western fear and ignorance of their possible consequences. Whereas he is popularly cited as the founder of *dialectical materialism* (which is usually described as a psychological view of man's basic greedy desire for material and monetary wealth), this is not exactly what he had in mind, nor is it characterized as such in any of his numerous works. Rather, he employed the *dialectical method* to study human history and existence, the fundamental conditions of which have, in his mind, a *materialistic* basis (materialistic in the philosophical sense, not in the sense of possessions or money). He declared himself a *realistic humanist* who recognized not the abstract and speculative concerns of man but the practical and obvious problems of existence. From this, he advanced the theory that the primary concerns and problems of man can be reduced to the very elementary conditions of existence (the food-shelter-clothing maxim, as it were), and that these conditions were the proper objects for study in attempting to define and improve the situation of man in the world. In other words, whereas most philosophy deals with man's *ideal* situation (his ideas and the problems arising therefrom), Marx's deals with man's real situation (his basic economic and social problems). He declared that the way in which man produces his means of subsistence is his most important

**117**

activity and is the expression of his life. As individuals express their life, *so they are*. The nature of the individual, then, is shaped by the material conditions that determine not only the way in which he exists, but also the way in which he *subsists*. He believed that his philosophy was neither exclusively idealism nor materialism, but a synthesis—*humanistic realism*. While idealist philosophy declares that ideas determine the existence of man, Marx held that the existence of man determines his ideas, and that this existence is, in reality, shaped by the dynamics of economic change in societies. Key works: *Economic and Philosophical Manuscripts* (1844); *German Ideology*, with Moses Hess (1846); *The Misery of Philosophy* (1847); *Capital*, vol. I. (1867), vols. II & III (1885, 1894), last two completed by Engels.

**Matthew of Aquasparta** (c. 1235-1302). A Franciscan priest and philosopher, he became a cardinal of the Church. He is noteworthy for his attempt to establish a reconciliation between the philosophies of PLATO and ARISTOTLE at a time when the systems of both were furiously divided. Plato, he said, tried to advance wisdom without knowledge, while Aristotle tried to foster knowledge without wisdom. Philosophy's real task, he declared, was to arrive at wisdom through knowledge and at faith through reason. Following AUGUSTINE's dictum, he claimed that in order to grasp ultimate truths, man must first understand the immediate truths of existence.

**Mazzini, Giuseppe** (1805-1872). An Italian political philosopher, he was born at Genoa. He conceived and tried to put into practice the grandiose idea of uniting Europe into a consolidated family of nations. A severe critic of nationalism, which he felt was at the root of the world's travails, his ultimate goal was to bring all the nations of mankind into a United Republic of the World. This idea, an enlargement of PLATO's Republic on a global scale, was regarded as dangerous and radical. As a result, Mazzini was considerably persecuted by various governments throughout Europe.

**Mead, George Herbert** (1863-1931). A distinguished professor of philosophy at the Univ. of Chicago, and a co-thinker and friend of DEWEY. Trained in biology and psychology, he emphasized in his philosophy the relationship of the individual to his own organic nature, as against the relationship of the individual to his society. Key work: *Philosophy of the Act* (1938).

**Meinong, Alexius** (1853-1920). Austrian psychological thinker. Originally a disciple of BRENTANO, he invented what he claimed was a new science — the *theory of objects*. For him, anything *intended* by thought is an object; objects may either *exist* (physical things) or *subsist* (facts, ideas); objects are apprehended either by *self-evident* judgments or by *imaginary* judgments (assumptions). This theory was devised to bridge what he considered to be the gap of inquiry into reality left by the other philosophical sciences. Key work: *Inquiry Into Object Theory and Psychology* (1904).

**Mencius** (372-289 B. C.). Born Meng-tse in what is now Shantung, China, he became the greatest exponent of Confucianism in ancient China. He vigorously attacked the teachings of the Taoists. After travelling, like CONFUCIUS, for many years in order to persuade kings and princes to practice benevolent government, and failing, he retired to write and study. He was concerned with practical ethics rather than abstract metaphysics.

**Mendelssohn, Moses** (1729-1786). German-Jewish philosopher who was born at Dessau. He achieved much popularity in his time and was the first to advocate the social emancipation of the Jews in Germany. A contemporary of KANT, who admired him, he specialized in psychology and aesthetics, but is best known for his defense of the immortality of the soul and of the existence of a personal God. Key work: *Evidence in Metaphysics* (1763).

**Mill, John Stuart** (1806-1873). Born in London, he died at Avignon, France. He was the son of the writer James Mill, who personally educated him. At the age of 3 he learned Greek; at 7 he studied PLATO; at 15 he was initiated by his father into the doctrines of BENTHAM (the greatest happiness of the greatest number), and became a confirmed utilitarian himself. He went on to refine this with French positivism and became England's leading social and political philosopher. In logic and the science of knowledge, he was a thoroughgoing *empiricist* (i.e. experience is the sole source of knowledge), and devised five *inductive* methods for comprehending the causal relations between objective phenomena. These were based on his advocacy of the law of the uniformity of nature. He defines the cause of an event as the sum total of its necessary conditions, positive and negative (i.e. if a plant needs water, dirt, and sunshine to grow from seed, but at the same time must be protected from frost and be given a certain amount of shade — these in their totality constitute the causes of the plant's growth). Key works: *System of Logic* (1843); *Essay on Liberty* (1859); *Utilitarianism* (1861).

**Molinos, Miguel de** (c. 1640-1697). Spanish philosopher born at Patacina, near Saragossa. He founded the philosophy of *Quietism* — a form of mysticism that sought quiet communion with the divine by means of a surrender of the mind to the influence of God.

**Montague, William Pepperell** (1873-1953). Born at Chelsea, Massachusetts, and for many years a professor at Columbia Univ., he was among the early leaders of American *new realism* in metaphysics. He maintained that reality exists

120

independent of and apart from consciousness, and that truth is independent of whether or not it is borne out in practice. Religiously, he was a *theist* (i.e. God exists and works in and through the world; this is the only milieu in which God can be apprehended). He felt that religion is valid only insofar as it is critical and does not exist on the basis of blind faith. Key work: *The Ways of Knowing, or the Methods of Philosophy* (1925).

**Montaigne, Michel de** (1533-1592). Born at Périgord, he was a notable French philosophical essayist who doubted the possibility of knowledge being certain (viz. his famous question: "What do I know") and recommended a return to nature and revelation. He is famous for his popular, common-sense insights into human nature. Key work: *Essays* (1580-1588).

**Montesquieu, Charles de Secondat de** (1689-1755). Born near Bordeaux, France, he was, along with LOCKE, the most important political and social philosopher of his time, and his writings were a strong influence behind both the French and American Revolutions. He advocated the separation of the various powers of government — or the *system of checks and balances* that is a major aspect of the American Constitution. He also made important studies of the historical and philosophical origins of law and government. Key works: *Persian Letters* (1721); *Spirit of the Laws* (1748).

**Moore, George Edward** (1873-1958). Born at London. G. E. Moore is a leading exponent of British *new realism* and had a long career as a professor of logic at Cambridge Univ. A vigorous opponent of idealism, he felt that knowledge is obtained not through ideas but through the actual confrontation of the mind with the objects of reality. He is also important for his work in ethical theory. He fostered the *emotive theory of value* (i.e. things cannot be valued by virtue of anything else but their intrinsic properties). By this, all ethical theories — whether metaphysical, utilitarian, subjective, or what — are invalid because they attempt to discover or derive the value of things from the mind, rather than objectively from the things themselves as they exist. In other words, for Moore, the proper way of valuing is to *attach* value rather than to *derive* it; that is, to perceive things as best we can, and then, based on the emotions their indefinable properties evoke in us, to approve or disapprove them. Key works: *Refutation of Idealism in Mind* (1903); *Principia Ethica* (1908).

**More, Thomas** (1478-1535). Born in London, he eventually became Lord Chancellor of the Crown. He was subsequently beheaded for his refusal to recognize the king as head of the Church. A pious Catholic, it was as a humanistic political and social thinker that he is important to philosophy. He advocated the formation of an ideal, democratic state in which the ruler and all magistrates would be elected, nothing would be private, all work and leisure would be shared, and neither oppression nor war would be possible. Main work: *Utopia* (1516).

**Morgan, C. Lloyd** (1852-1936). English biologist who attempted a synthesis of philosophy and science. As a philosopher, he was a *realist;* he felt, in accordance with modern physics, that all things were nothing but "clusters of events." He described the life process in terms of *emergent evolution* — a process of selective synthesis at certain critical turning points in the course of evolutionary advance — as against DARWIN's conception of evolution as a steady, gradual process. Key work: *Emergent Evolution* (1923).

**Mo Tzu** (c. 470-396 B. C.). Also known as Mo Ti and the founder of Mohism in ancient China, he was an accomplished militarist and statesman. He disavowed Confucianism for its doc-

122

trine of fate and for its elaborate rituals. He stressed purity of the heart over formal observance of ceremonial laws and argued that *universal love* is the true rule of existence.

**Münsterberg, Hugo** (1863-1916). German philosopher and psychologist, he was born at Danzig; he later emigrated to the U. S. and became a professor of psychology at Harvard Univ. Influenced by FICHTE and KANT, he advanced a theory of *intuitionism* which held that pure reason is endowed naturally with *a priori* principles. These enable it to achieve objective truths; however, these truths cannot be confirmed by psychological investigation. Key works: *Psychology and Doctrine* (1906); *External Values* (1908).

# N

**Nagel, Ernst** (1901- ). Born at Novemesto, Czechoslovakia, he emigrated to the U. S. (1911) and has become one of America's important contemporary philosophers. Mainly concerned with the philosophy of science, he wrote, with MORRIS COHEN, *An Introduction to Logic and the Scientific Method* (1934), which has become a standard work in the field. His thought is based on *naturalism* (i.e. the universe is made up merely of forces which require no explanation; these forces are uncontrolled and express no will or purpose). He repudiates all doctrines of *idealism;* in fact, all non-materialistic doctrines.

**Natorp, Paul** (1854-1924). German philosopher and psychologist born at Düsseldorf. He was a faithful follower of the philosophy of HERMANN COHEN and a collaborator in the Marburg School at the Univ. of Marburg. He espoused the *transcendental method* of knowledge (i.e. because of the existence of *a priori* principles or categories of knowledge, all things knowable are knowable by reason) and used this method to justify PLATO's doctrine of Universal Ideas. Key works: *Plato's Doctrine of Ideas* (1903); *Kant and the Marburg School* (1915).

**Newton, Isaac** (1642-1727). Renowned English mathematician and physicist who, in his classic *Mathematical Principles of Natural Philosophy* (1685-87), not only announced his discovery of the Law of Gravity but also presented a new system of mechanics by which the structure of the system of the universe was to be understood. He sought the true mechanical laws of nature not on the basis of *a priori* principles but on the basis of the most precise observation of phenomena in nature. One of the important consequences of this work lay in his development of the proper methods of reasoning; he claimed that philosophy's error in seeking the nature of reality was in its insistence on making deductions from phenomena without knowing first the causes of phenomena. He thus developed *five rules of reasoning* that disallowed the concept of *hypothesis*—always a primary and necessary characteristic of philosophical thinking. He insisted that the only way to get at the true causes of things is to scientifically observe, observe, observe, until, through such a totality of observation, the causes of things make themselves known.

**Nicholas of Cusa.** See Cusa.

**Nicolai, Friedrich** (1733-1811). A German contemporary of KANT and FICHTE who suffered considerable critical abuse at the hands of both. He was a *common sense* thinker whose distrust of the sophisticated systematization of formal philosophy, coupled with his tendency to select the best features of various philosophies for his own, earned him the scorn of most of his fellow thinkers. Key work: *Long Lost Philosophies* (1808).

**Nietzsche, Friedrich** (1844-1900). Born at Röcken in Saxony, he was an important German psychological philosopher who strove to divest philosophy of hypocritical and dishonest postures and to invest it with the function of realistic prophecy. Basing his views on an admiration of Zoroastrianism and early Greek culture, he examined the evolution of morals and found it shot through with the psychological failings of human thought. He declared that the highest values in religion and morals had lost their influence; to correct this, he developed the concept of the *will to power* (i.e. the ruling principle of all life, organic or inorganic, is the instinct to achieve eminence and authority). He posited this as the ultimate and absolute value of life. It is the function of philosophy, then, to realize this value and to guide man to the attainment of it. Once man attains it, or at least a segment of mankind does, he will use it to purify and perfect himself. The political implications of this doctrine have been considered dangerous, especially in view of Adolph Hitler's successful distortion of it in Nazi Germany. Key works: *Thus Spake Zarathustra* (1883-84); *Beyond Good and Evil* (1886); *The Genealogy of Morals.*

**Noüy, Pierre Lecomte du** (1883-1947). French thinker who developed a novel philosophical theory of evolution operating on three parallel planes — *biological, psychical,* and *moral.* He held that the psychical and moral phases of evolution progress more rapidly than the biological phase. The fact that the two spiritual phases advance more rapidly than the material phase substantiates the validity of religion and ethics in that they reflect the effort of man to collaborate with God to produce a better world. Key work: *Human Destiny* (1947).

**Nuñes-Regüeiro, Manuel** (1883- ). Born in Uruguay, he became an important Argentine ethical philosopher whose thought is based on three questions: What can I know? What must I do? What can I expect? He felt that life consists basically of chaos, at the root of which lies a *crisis of values.* The resolution of this crisis will put life in order, and only through the search for values does man give life meaning — by attempting to effect such a resolution. Key work: *Metaphysics and Science* (1941).

# O

**Ockham, William of** (1280-1348). English Christian thinker born at Ockham in Surrey. He repudiated much of the widely accepted doctrines of AQUINAS and AUGUSTINE, especially as such doctrines related to justifying the Church's supreme position in the temporal affairs of men. Philosophically, he proclaimed the primacy of logic in all disciplines and insisted on the *nominalistic* doctrine that universals are not real but are simply terms. In line with this, he further insisted that things *not known* to exist should not, unless absolutely necessary, be postulated as existing — in his words, "The number of entities should not be needlessly increased." He further declared that no theological doctrines are evident or demonstrable by means of logic, so they must rest solely on faith. Key work: *Summa Totius Logicae.*

**Origen** (184-253). Born at Alexandria, Egypt, he was the principal creator of Christian dogmatic theology. He studied under CLEMENT OF ALEXANDRIA and attempted to integrate the early Christian notion of God into a comprehensive explanation of the universe, based on PLATO's doctrine of Ideas. He lived a life of total asceticism and is reputed to have written over 600 works. He introduced into Christianity many ideas that later formed the basis for more complex and sophisticated dogmas (e.g. the Trinity). He also pragmatically declared that belief in Christ is worthwhile because such belief had a beneficial effect on the believers.

129

**Ortega y Gasset, José** (1883-1955). Born in Madrid, Spain, he lived his later years in exile in Argentina because of his opposition to the Franco government. After an early Jesuit education, he studied at the Central Univ. of Madrid, where he subsequently became a professor of metaphysics following further studies at the Universities of Leipzig, Berlin and Marburg. Although a student of HERMANN COHEN at Marburg, where he was saturated with the *critical idealism* of KANT, he later became an opponent of idealism. He claimed life to be more important than thought; because life is ever-shifting and mutating, a proper understanding of man demands the abandonment of the immobile concepts postulated by logical theory and the development of mobile thinking processes. To him, the conceptual reality posited by idealism is not reality at all: reality is to be found in history, especially in personal history (i.e. in the individual's autobiography). Thus, history considered through reason is the proper approach to reality; the two are co-existent conditions for truth. Hence, reality does not consist in Being, but rather in Becoming, for what does the rational consideration of history demonstrate except the eternal, evolutionary process of things in nature? Key works: *The Theme of Our Time* (1923); *Kant* (1924); *Ideas and Beliefs* (1940).

**Ostwald, Wilhelm** (1853-1932). Born at Riga, Germany, this chemist and philosopher won the Nobel Prize for Chemistry (1909). His philosophy advocates, in opposition to materialism, the doctrine of *energy* as the principle of all life. This doctrine was based on his view that the properties of matter are all special forms of energy; hence, it is from a kind of *Universal Energy* that all things derive their existence. Key works: *Nature Philosophy* (1902); *Energy* (1908).

# P

**Paley, William** (1743-1805). English theologian who was born at Peterborough and died at Lincoln, England. He made contributions to the field of ethics. As an advocate of the ethical doctrine of *expediency* (i.e. those actions are best that are most beneficial), he influenced the rise of utilitarianism. He based this doctrine upon his conception that man's happiness is a divine law. Key work: *Principles of Moral and Political Philosophy* (1785).

**Palmer, George Herbert** (1842-1933). Born at Boston, he was a significant American philosopher of ethics. He was a professor of philosophy at Harvard and died at Cambridge, Massachusetts. He devoted his thought to clarifying the idea of "the good" in ethics. The soul, he declared, is not content merely to be good; it feels impelled "to be good for something" — for social activity as opposed to personal gain. Key works: *The Nature of Goodness* (1901); *The Problem of Freedom* (1911).

**Panaetius of Rhodes** (c. 180-110 B. C.). Greek philosopher of *stoicism*. He admired Plato and belittled theological dogmatism. To him, the point of philosophy was moral reflection, and he infused stoicism with a resolutely humanistic coloration. He declared that man is the center of the universe and that he is at once a natural being and a cultural (artificial) being — an irreducible dualism upon which morality is founded. If man's wisdom consists of knowing and acting according to his nature, man must respect in himself that which defines him as man — his humanity.

**Papini, Giovanni** (1881-1956). Italian philosopher who was born and died at Florence. A *pragmatist*, he held that the fact of human progress points to a purposeful aim in man's activities — an ethical and therefore practical endeavor to establish fellowship throughout the world. Key work: *The Finished Man* (1913).

**Paracelsus, Theophrastus Bombast** (1493-1541). Medieval German physician who endeavored to use philosophy as a pillar of medical science. His thought is a disparate combination of PLATO's idealism and magic superstition. Key work: *On the Nature of Things.*

**Pareto, Vilfredo** (1848-1923). Born in Paris, he later settled in Switzerland and became a professor of political economy at the Univ. of Lausanne. An admirer of MACHIAVELLI, he advocated *absolute government* as the only form of government practicable for human society, and expressed himself in cynical terms regarding the humanitarian aspects of democracy. He declared that the minority should rule as severe masters and that the majority should serve as obedient subjects. His philosophy had great attraction for the Italian Fascists, who heaped honors upon him and endeavored to make him their official spokesman. Key works: *Manual of Political Economics* (1906); *The Mind and Society* (1916).

**Parmenides** (c. 504-456 B. C.). Founder of the *Eleatic* school of ancient Greek philosophy and one of the very important Greek thinkers. Born in Elea, in what is now Southern Italy, he resided for some years in Athens. He was the originator of the doctrine of *being*, which he developed in opposition to the doctrine of *becoming* of HERACLITUS. He also initiated the distinction between a sensible world (the world known

132

by the senses) and an intelligible world (the world known by the mind). He declared, through logical reasoning, that thought is the same as being, and that being is one and constitutes reality. He denied the possibility of non-being by reason of the fact that since being is the same as thought, to think at all we must think of something that has being — something that *is*. That which has no being — that which *is not* — cannot be thought. Therefore, it is impossible for something to *not be*. It follows then that all things perceived, either through the senses or through the mind, must exist.

**Pascal, Blaise** (1623-1662). French philosopher, mathematician and physicist who made great contributions to science through his studies in hydrodynamics and the mathematical theory of probability. Dissatisfied with experimentation, he turned to the study of man and his spiritual problems. He produced a religion-oriented philosophy that concerned itself primarily with the relation of man to God through religion and faith. He regarded truth as the expression of God's will and as a means of knowing God. Although he felt reason to be a sound faculty of man, he declared faith to be a sounder guide to truth. He was the author of the famous phrase: "The heart has its reasons that the reason does not know." Key work: *Pensées*.

**Patanjali** (c. 200 B. C.). Hindu philosopher who invented the philosophical system of *Yoga*. The adherents of this system submit themselves to the yoke (*yoga*-yoke) of discipline and abstinence in order to cleanse their spirits of all material corruptions and to achieve supernatural wisdom. Key work: *Yoga Sutra*.

**Pater, Walter Horatio** (1839-1894). English philosopher of *hedonism* (which advocates a life of rationally refined pleasure) and *humanism* (i.e. the sole concern of man is man). The essence of his thought lies in his conviction that life, which is nothing but a sharply defined present moment between two unmeaningful eternities, is secure and intelligible to man, and that the art of living consists in the ability to make such a passing moment yield the utmost of enjoyment. He tried to show that devotion to pleasure gives the soul a strength and austerity that cannot be surpassed, even by moral uprightness. Key works: *Renaissance* (1873); *Marius the Epicurean* (1885).

**Peano, Giuseppe** (1858-1932). Italian mathematician and professor of mathematics at the Univ. of Turin (1890-1932). He made several contributions to mathematical logic, especially in his efforts to renounce common language and to shape an instrument of language that would render to thought the same services the microscope renders to biology — his system permits the writing of every proposition in logic in symbols exclusively, in order to emancipate the strict logical part of reasoning from verbal language and its vagueness. Key work: *Elements of Geometrical Calculus* (1886).

**Peirce, Charles Sanders** (1839-1914). American philosopher born at Cambridge, Mass., and educated at Harvard. Except for occasional and brief lecturing assignments at Harvard and Johns Hopkins Universities, he did no formal teaching and was little known during his lifetime. Other philosophers brought him recognition by acknowledging his importance to pragmatic philosophy. He in fact initiated the doctrine of *pragmatism* (the ascertaining of the meaning and value of an intellectual conception by considering the sum of the consequences which would result from the practical application of that conception). He developed this doctrine as a method of logical analysis; it was later defined differently by JAMES and DEWEY. His pragmatism was based on his earlier theory of *fallibilism* (i.e. truth is only provisional and not absolute, and the *probability* exists that anything which is advanced as a truth can be contradicted). From this assumption he proceeded to the conviction that theoretical truth, because it is fallible and therefore only probable, must constantly be tested in practical experience. He also claimed that there is an inseparable connection between rational *cognition* and rational *purpose,* and that there is thus and likewise a close relation between thought and conduct. Key work: *Grand Logic.*

**Perry, Ralph Barton** (1876-1957). An American thinker born at Poultney, Vermont, he was long a professor at Harvard and one of the founders of American *new realism.* He later departed from this movement and devoted his studies to a kind of humanistic theology in which *freedom* was postulated as the prime attribute of men, to be cultivated and developed militantly, both through the individual and through his society. Also: Man has everything to gain and nothing to lose by subscribing to a belief in God and immortality; he should therefore take this *hazard of faith,* for all life is a gamble and the best gamble of all is for eternal life. Key works: *General Theory of Value* (1926); *Shall Not Perish From the Earth* (1941).

**Philo** (c. 30 B. C.-50 A. D.). A Jewish theologian and neo-Platonic philosopher, he lived most of his life in Alexandria, Egypt. He justified his use of Greek thought for the purpose of Biblical interpretation by declaring that Greek thought borrowed largely from ancient Jewish teachings. He was the first thinker to introduce into philosophy the problem of reconciling speculative and rational thought with religious faith and revelation. (This problem, of course, became one of philosophy's major concerns throughout its history). His primary philosophical view was that the mind is capable, by *intuition,* rather than by reasoning, to affirm the existence of God, although it cannot understand His nature. From this, he proceeded to develop a strong *monotheistic mysticism.*

135

**Pico della Mirandola, Giovanni** (1463-1494). A nobleman and philosopher of the early Renaissance in Italy, he sought to synthesize the thought of ARISTOTLE and PLATO and, in fact, to reconcile all philosophies which, according to him, conflicted with one another only through appearance. The principal philosophical view that compelled him to seek this reconciliation was based on the doctrine of *unity in diversity* (i.e. there are many beings, but they are all an integral part of one Being). He at one time planned to challenge all scholars of the world by defending 900 of his theses in a public debate at Rome (1487), but the Church prevented him from doing so and condemned him for 13 of his conclusions. Key work: *On Being and One.*

**Plato** (427-347 B. C.). Born on the island of Aegina, a colony of Athens, he was one of the most enduring of the ancient Greek philosophers. Originally known as Aristocles, he was given the best education available and spent eight years as a student of SOCRATES. He acquired a broad knowledge of pre-Socratic philosophies (e.g. THALES, HERACLITUS, PARMENIDES, etc.) and founded his own school in Athens (387). He taught at the Platonic Academy until his death. His philosophy represents one of the great and lasting strains of thought in history, and still remains of major significance and influence. The entire construction of his thought is based upon his conception of true reality as a world of *Ideas.* These Ideas, or Forms (the terms are used interchangeably), are universal, immaterial *essences* that contain the true and ultimate realities (being) of things, while the actual world of sensible things (things perceivable by the senses) is only a vague, transitory and untrustworthy copy. Thus, since the function of thought is to perceive reality, its function becomes precisely to perceive the world of Ideas. Only the cognition of Ideas, or of the Universal Forms, enables man to perfect himself and to act with wisdom. In line with this view, Plato criticizes reliance on knowledge gained through the senses because the objects of the senses exist only as imperfect manifestations of the Universal Forms (Ideas) that comprise their essences; such knowledge, therefore, is itself imperfect — in his words, *opinion, not truth*. Through the reasoned exercise of the mind, however, man is able to arrive at true knowledge via the rational perception of the Universals (Forms, Ideas) that contain the essence of all sensible, material things. The mind is able to perceive the Universal Ideas by virtue of the fact that the mind has its own Universal Idea (i.e. there is a Universal Mind that contains the essence of all finite and individual minds). Plato states further that within the world of Universal Ideas there is a certain hierarchy. The Idea of Good is at the top, and all other Ideas participate in it and derive from it, just as all material objects participate in and derive from their own Universal Ideas. The Idea of Good, being the ultimate Idea, permeates all things. The relation, then, of man to ultimate reality (The Universal Ideas) is basically an imitative one (i.e. man should mentally perceive and imitate the perfection of the Universal Idea of himself). Although there are contradictions and unresolved conflicts in Plato's system, especially as it relates to the various subdivisions of philosophy (ethics, metaphysics, etc.), and although his system has never been able to be worked out to the total satisfaction of logic, it is a grand design that has had profound, lasting and valid significance. His method is best defined as a dialectic, in that he demonstrated his arguments by *opposition*. He believed in the unity of opposites, and it is said by some that the dialectical style in which his works were written is the true reflection of his philosophy — that reality consists in the unity of opposites and that the cognition of this unity constitutes knowledge of reality. Main works: *Republic; Symposium; Phaedrus; Phaedo; Theaetetus; Protagoras; Timaeus; Apology; Crito.*

**Plotinus** (205-270). Born in Egypt, he lived and taught in Rome for over 25 years, and died there. At first a pagan, he became an authority on and advocate of the philosophy of India, as well as the idealism of PLATO. He based his thought on the theory that the material reality *perceived* by the senses is of a lower order and value than spiritual reality *conceived* by the mind, which is the true reality. He maintained a hierarchy of reality, each less than the next in value, and all emanating from the ultimate *One*. *Mind* (*nous*) and *soul* (*psyche*) emanate directly from the *One*, while further down the ladder is matter, then material objects. Since man participates in all these emanations, he is a composite of spirit and matter. Because of this, sense knowledge is virtually valueless in the quest for truth, since that which the senses are capable of knowing (material objects) are of a lower order and value than the sensory agent (man). Thus, very much like the Universals of Plato, his reality consists of Intelligible Ideas and is headed by the Idea of Beauty, which is the *One*. The climax of knowledge consists in an intuitive and mystical union with the *One*. Main work: *Enneads*.

**Poincaré, Henri** (1854-1912). French mathematician and physicist born at Nancy. His main contribution to philosophy stemmed from his inquiry into logic, in which he specifically questioned the validity of making hypotheses. From the statement that for any consistent and verifiable hypotheses or definitions there can be found other equally consistent and verifiable hypotheses or definitions, he proceeded to the conclusion that the choice between them is not dictated by logic or observation but by what he called *convention* (i.e. accepting them because of tradition). Hypotheses of the type described by the statement above were known as *logical paradoxes;* to solve the problem of these paradoxes he proposed that in defining a thing of a certain type or class, no reference should be made to the totality of things of that type or class. In other words, a definition of a thing should limit itself only to that particular thing, and should not compare the thing being defined to other things, even of the same type. Definitions that did not observe this principle he called *unpredicative definitions* (definitions having no predicate, or lacking in descriptive quality). Key works: *Science and Hypothesis* (1902); *Science and Method* (1909).

**Pomponazzi, Pietro** (1462-1525). Born at Mantua, Italy, he studied medicine and philosophy and later taught at the Universities of Padua, Ferrara and Bologna. Living in a time (the Italian Renaissance) when the philosophy of ARISTOTLE was being abandoned and that of PLATO revived, he remained a staunch Aristotelian. He denied that Aristotle had propounded the personal immortality of the soul (which Scholastic philosophy had maintained and which Renaissance thinkers had objected to) and himself disavowed belief in such immortality. He fostered the importance of human experience in the quest for truth and, in criticizing religion, declared that human experience was alone sufficient to compel man to be good and virtuous. He concluded that man did not need unsubstantiated religious concepts to guide him. Main work: *On the Immortality of the Soul* (1516).

**Popper, Karl** (1902-    ). Born and educated at Vienna, and presently a professor of logic at the London School of Economics, he is important as a contemporary philosopher of science. A critic of FRANCIS BACON's *inductive method* of scientific reasoning, he has developed a form of reasoning based on *probability*. He starts by defining scientific statements as those which deny that something *logically conceivable* is *actually realized*. According to this definition, a statement is not necessarily scientific just because it can be confirmed by experience; it is essential for such a statement to be capable of being disproved by some possible event which, were it to occur, would exemplify a possibility that the statement itself excludes. It is this feature of its statements that Popper thinks separates science from, say, metaphysics. Key work: *The Logic of Discovery* (1934).

**Porphyry** (232-304). A friend and disciple of PLOTINUS, he was born at Tyre in Africa. He adapted the principles of Aristotelian logic to his own form of idealism, and invented a method of classifying things by means of *dichotomy* (i.e. analysis of a thing through analysis of its parts), known as the *Tree of Porphyry*. Key work: *The Return of the Soul.*

**Posidonius** (c. 135-50 B. C.). Born on the island of Rhodes, he was the most significant and original exponent of later Greek *Stoic* philosophy. He incorporated into his thought many doctrines of PLATO and ARISTOTLE. To him, being was identical with the cosmos, reality was a giant organism that spun off from being, and *fire* was the essence of being. Key work: *Protracted Discourses.*

**Proclus** (411-485). Born in Constantinople, he was a prominent neo-Platonic thinker who taught that man becomes united with God through the practice of love, truth and faith. Key work: *Ten Doubts About Providence.*

**Protagoras** (c. 485-410 B. C.). The leading *Sophist* philosopher of the ancient Greek period, he was born at Abdera and lived for awhile in Athens. He was forced to flee Athens under sentence of death after having been accused of impiety. (The Sophist philosophers were for many centuries unjustly discredited in philosophy because of the influence of PLATO, who branded them as dishonest thinkers and teachers who would readily teach falsehood for money). A disciple of DEMOCRITUS, he espoused the doctrine of *atomistic materialism* (i.e. reality consists of atoms, and the variety of atomic forms accounts for the variety of material things in the world). He claimed that sensation was the only source of knowledge; however, since knowledge is *in* any particular

140

sensation, man is capable of knowing only what his senses tell him about what he perceives, not the thing itself perceived. Thus, sense knowledge is incomplete and not to be trusted, and man is wiser to be skeptical about everything. From this came his famous formula: *Man is the measure of all things.*

**Proudhon, Pierre Joseph** (1809-1864). Born at Besançon, France, he was an important social philosopher and economist. He believed — like Marx later — that the function of philosophy is *not to interpret* the world *but to alter it.* He was strongly *socialistic* in his outlook and spent three years in prison (1849-52) because of his radical statements. He based his socialism on his concept of *property* — "property is theft" — and advocated a share and share-alike system between capital and labor. Key work: *The Philosophy of Poverty* (1846).

**Ptah-Hotep** (c. 2800 B. C.). Often considered the first philosopher in history (see URAKAGINA), he was an Egyptian statesman and an advisor to Pharaohs. The first thinker to record the idea of the *resurrection of the soul,* he also declared a belief in *one God.* The entirety of his thought reflected the practical aspects of philosophy and life, and he was an ancient precursor of modern pragmatism.

**Pyrrho** (c. 365-275 B. C.). Greek thinker from Elis. He was a systematic skeptic who believed that it is impossible to know the true nature of things, and that the wise man suspends judgment on all matters and seeks to attain simple happiness by abstaining from passion and curiosity.

**Pythagoras** (c. 572-510 B. C.). Eminent Greek mathematician and philosopher. He was born, most probably, on the island of Samos. He emigrated (c. 538 B. C.) to Southern Italy, where he taught and established the Pythagorean school. His philosophy was based upon a *dualism* that sharply distinguished between thought and the senses, between soul and body, and between the *forms of things* and their *perceptible appearances*. Much of his thought has been mixed with that of his disciples. They extended his ideas into a conception of reality in which numbers are the substance of all things, and all things perceived in the world are sensible expressions of mathematical ratios. Thus, for them, reality consisted of a mathematical harmony of number. For instance, in the relation between odd and even numbers is seen a corollary to the relation between body and soul, and all other dualistic conceptions. Pythagoras' philosophy had a marked influence on the development of PLATO's idealistic conception of reality.

# R

**Ramakrishna, Sri** (1836-1886). The most influential of the 19th century thinkers in India, he was born at Kamurpukur. He developed the doctrine of *samadhi* (i.e. God can be known through a heightened state of consciousness brought about by contemplation), and claimed to have experienced a divine communion with the "Mother of the Universe." His thought was impelled by his belief that the world we live in is a world of *illusion;* that man lives in a mist of false observations and distorted images, and cannot be happy until he is able to use his mind, in an elevated way, to cut though the deceptions of his senses.

**Ramanuja** (c. 1220-1280). Renowned Indian thinker who assumed the world and the soul to be a transformation of God into the natural realm.

**Ramsey, Frank Plumpton** (1903-1930). English mathematical philosopher whose premature death terminated a brief but brilliant career. Expanding upon the logical problems raised by RUSSELL and WITTGENSTEIN, he made a fundamental distinction between *human* logic, which deals with useful mental habits and is applicable to the realm of practical probability, and *formal* logic, which is concerned exclusively with the rules of consistent thought. Key work: *The Foundations of Mathematics* (1930).

**Ravaisson-Mollien, Jean** (1813-1900). French idealist philosopher, he was born at Namur and studied under SCHELLING at the Univ. of Munich, later becoming a professor of philosophy at Rennes (1838). Although he wrote little, he profoundly influenced French philosophy in the direction of *dynamic spiritualism* (i.e. universal concepts such as cause, substance, etc., are manifestations of the directly experienced activity of the human will). Key works: *On the Metaphysics of Aristotle* (1837-46); *On Habit* (1839).

**Reichenbach, Hans** (1891-1953). German scientific philosopher born at Hamburg. He taught, first, engineering at the Univ. of Stuttgart, then philosophy at the Universities of Berlin, Istanbul and California (Los Angeles). He developed a general theory of *probability* based on a statistical definition of the concept of probability (roughly: *probability,* or the chance of something happening, can be arithmetically calculated). From this, he was able to analyze events and other phenomena of reality and obtain *positive,* or affirmative, knowledge with respect to their probable truth. Key work: *Experience and Prediction* (1938).

**Reid, Thomas** (1710-1796). Scottish philosopher who was born at Strachan and died at Glasgow. He opposed the spiritualistic and idealistic tradition of BERKELEY and HUME and declared instead that man has a common consciousness, or *common sense,* that enables him to know truth through self-evidence. Thus, our common sense informs us that the external world exists, that there is a cause and effect relationship in the world, that there is a definite law of human conduct, and that we have immortal souls. Main work: *Inquiry into the Mind on the Principles of Common Sense.*

**Renouvier, Charles** (1818-1903). French philosopher born at Montpelier. He followed in the critical tradition of KANT and FICHTE but denied the existence of transcendental entities such as the *thing-in-itself,* the *Absolute,* etc. To him, everything in knowledge can be reduced to its *representation* (i.e. we can only know the representation of things — their physical characteristics, etc. — not the things in themselves). This outlook led him to postulate the doctrine of *phenomenalism* (i.e. there is no difference between objective nature and subjective knowledge; instead, all phenomena in nature are representations, and they represent themselves *at once,* not in stages. Thus, what we know of a thing we know at once, not in stages). Key works: *General Critical Essays* (1851-64); *Analytical Philosophy of History* (1896-98); *The New Monadology* (1899).

**Rickert, Heinrich** (1863-1936). German thinker, he was born at Danzig and later taught philosophy at the Univ. of Heidelberg (1916-36). He fought against efforts to limit the concept and function of science exclusively to the natural sciences. He demonstrated that natural sciences could form only limited concepts, concepts dealing with just part of nature; other sciences, namely historical and philosophical, were necessary to deal with that aspect of reality that natural science could not encompass. This neglected aspect of reality is, according to him, the realm of values; value cannot be explained or validated by natural sciences — it needs history to go beyond mere fact-gathering to the discovery of general laws about it, and philosophy to seek absolute cultural interpretations of these laws. He concluded, then, that value is the philosophical aspect of reality. Key work: *Culture and Nature* (1899).

**Ritschl, Albrecht** (1822-1889). German Christian thinker who established a school of thought which argued that God can be known on the basis of what he conceived of as the *religious value judgment.* Such a judgment is demonstrated as follows: God is responsible for the death of every individual; the individual knows this; yet the individual still seeks and

145

trusts God. By so doing, the individual admits to God's existence and has a way by which he can approach God rationally. Key work: *Theology and Metaphysics: Their Understanding and Defense* (1874).

**Romero, Francisco** (1891-  ). Born in Spain, he has become a leading South American philosopher. He taught philosophy at the Universities of Buenos Aires and La Plata. He followed KORN both in philosophical outlook and in his endeavor to advance an Argentinian philosophical tradition. Continuing the opposition to *positivism* and *rationalism,* he has developed a *structural conception of reality* (i.e. reality is a kind of edifice of beings, held together by transcendent True Being). Key works: *Old and New Conception of Reality* (1932); *Theory and Practice of Truth* (1939).

**Roscelin** (c. 1050-1120). Born at Compiègne, France, he was the teacher of ABELARD. He is noted in philosophy for his doctrine of *nominalism* (the theory that abstract or general terms, or universals, do not represent objective realities but are simply words or names; thus, universals have no reality prior to the objects to which such reality is attached by the mind, and they exist only in the mind).

**Roshd, Mohammad ibn.** See AVERROËS.

**Ross, William David** (1877-1940). Born in England and known principally as an Aristotelian scholar, W. D. Ross served as the editor of the classic Oxford University translation into English of ARISTOTLE's works. Key work: *The Right and the Good* (1930).

**Rousseau, Jean Jacques** (1712-1778). French thinker, born in Geneva, Switzerland. His educational and political ideas especially had great influence in France and throughout Europe. Basically a philosopher of history and a critic of modern civilization, he condemned both as reflecting a deviation from the compelling truths of nature. His thought was centered in his concepts that every man is unique unto himself and all men are equal. Key work: *The Social Contract* (1762).

**Royce, Josiah** (1855-1916). Important American philosopher of metaphysics and logic. Born at Grass Valley, California, he was for many years a professor of philosophy at Harvard Univ. An *idealist* steeped in the philosophy of HEGEL, he first conceived of reality as an all-inclusive, absolute mind, of which our minds are fragmentary manifestations. He later revised this, substituting all-inclusive, absolute will for mind. He thus linked human experience to absolute experience, saying that the human *participates* in the Absolute; it is through this participation that man can understand all things. Absolute experience, although a closed and perfect whole, is shot through with imperfections, which themselves constitute the properties of human experience. Absolute experience struggles with these imperfections, and it is through this struggle and the eventual triumph over them that the Absolute achieves its own perfection. The struggle is represented on the human plane by the human compulsion (will) to know truth and perfection (participate in the Absolute). Hence, philosophical activity assumes the characteristics of religious activity: participation in the Ultimate. Key works: *The Religious Aspect of Philosophy* (1885); *The World and the Individual* (1900); *Lectures on Modern Idealism* (1919).

**Russell, Bertrand A.** (1872- ). Eminent English mathematical philosopher born at Trelleck. He has taught and lectured widely, and written voluminously. He is also a controversial public figure who has spent time in prison for his unpopular political views. Two aspects of his work are likely to remain of permanent importance: (1) his major contribution to modern logic: (2) his attempts to identify the methods of philosophy with those of the sciences. He has played an outstanding role, with WHITEHEAD, in the foundation of modern mathematical logic. His fundamental position is that logic is not a function of philosophy but a general theory of science; further, that the proper function of philosophy is to deal with the problems raised by the sciences, not with theological or ethical problems. Hence, philosophy should devote itself to analyzing the empirical data of science, because the primary problem of human life consists in the relation between individual experience and general scientific knowledge. Knowledge itself is a relatively unimportant feature of the universe; it can also be a corruptive influence in the search for truth, since it is so subject to the interpretations of human experience. To counter this, philosophy must limit itself to simple, objective descriptions of the phenomena of the world, keeping such descriptions free of the self-same corrupt influences of experience. Key works: *Principia Mathematica* (*Principles of Mathematics*) 3 vols. (1910-1913); *The Problems of Philosophy* (1917); *Introduction to Mathematical Philosophy* (1918); *Inquiry into Meaning and Truth* (1940).

**Ryle, Gilbert** (1900-  ). Born at Brighton, he is a significant English philosopher whose main contributions to philosophy have been in refining the doctrines of *linguistic analysis* (i.e. the object of philosophy should be to first analyze the language in which concepts are stated before endeavoring to understand the concepts themselves). He held that the main task of philosophy is to solve problems caused by man's failure to understand the workings of the mind, and to discover whether certain "recurrent misconceptions" and absurd theories "stem from the misuse of language itself." Key work: *The Concept of Mind* (1949).

148

# S

**Saadia, Ben Joseph** (892-942). Jewish thinker who was born and educated in Egypt, and who settled in Babylonia (915). He specialized in many fields of learning; in philosophy, he tried to demonstrate that the principles of Judaism were compatible with reason. Key work: *Doctrines and Religious Beliefs.*

**Saint-Simon, Claude Henri** (1760-1825). French nobleman and social thinker who was born in Paris, he fought with the French army during the American Revolution. He advanced a new science of society that would do away with inequalities in the distribution of property, wealth and power. Love for the poor and lowly was the basic tenet of his doctrine for social reform. Key work: *Industrial Catechism* (1823-24).

**Santayana, George** (1863-1952). Important American philosopher who was born in Madrid, Spain. He was brought to the U. S. at the age of 9. He later studied at Harvard and taught philosophy there for many years afterwards. He spent the waning years of his life in study at a convent in Italy, where he continued to write. Initially a strong admirer of the idealism of PLATO, he developed his own influential doctrine of *materialistic naturalism* (i.e. the universe requires no supernatural cause, but is self-existent, self-sustaining and self-directing, with its source in matter). He declared that consciousness, instead of distorting the nature of reality, immediately reveals it (which was opposite to the conclusion of RUSSELL). To him, reality partially consists in an infinity of essences (universal forms) that eternally *subsist*. These essences begin to *exist* when they are naturally enacted upon by matter. Essences (ideas), then, are the perfect models of our imperfect images of the world; in experiencing an essence (idea) of a thing, as distinct from its image, we can perceive its reality. So then, essence precedes matter, but matter completes essence, and the human comprehension of this relation constitutes an understanding of the world. From this materialist-essentialist world-view, he proceeded to define Ultimate Reality as that in which the subsistent and existent essences form a harmonious whole. Key works: *Life of Reason,* 5 vols. (1905-1906); *Skepticism and Animal Faith* (1923); *Realms of Being,* 4 vols. (1927-40).

**Sartre, Jean Paul** (1905- ). A leading contemporary French philosopher and advocate of modern *existentialism,* he was born at Paris. Orphaned at a young age, he studied at the Sorbonne and later under HUSSERL at the Univ. of Göttingen in Germany. He was for awhile a prisoner of the Germans during World War II; upon his release he returned to Paris and became a leader in the French Resistance. His philosophy is deeply influenced by HUSSERL and HEIDEGGER. Described as existentialism, it is based on three root ideas: (1) Existence precedes essence (i.e. man is the sole creator of his own values, standards, principles and morality; truth does not exist except insofar as it is created by and refers to man; thus, there is no God; indeed, there is no source above man for the ideas he discovers and the values he adopts). (2) Man is profoundly unhappy that there is no God or other source above him. He is, as it were, condemned to freedom (i.e. a creature of anguish and despair by virtue of his having to exist alone in the world with nothing to relate himself to except himself; thus, man simply exists). (3) However, given this total and precarious state of freedom, man must deal with it, in fact, make the best of it. Hence, he must commit himself to an involvement in his condition and in his struggle to make the most and best of his freedom. Key works: *Being and Nothingness* (1943); *Existentialism As Humanism* (1946).

**Scheler, Max** (1874-1928). German philosopher. Originally a disciple of EUCKEN and of *spiritualism*, he later became, through the influence of HUSSERL, an advocate of *phenomenology* (which calls for purely descriptive analyses of the subjective perceptions of objects, events, etc., that occur in the world). His system was based on an assumption that a definite co-relation exists between the essences of objects and the essences of the mind. From this he concluded, among other things, that all knowledge derives from the interaction of these essences, and that knowledge is most truly rendered through straight description. Key work: *Philosophical World View* (1929).

**Schelling, Friedrich von** (1775-1854). German thinker who was born at Leonberg and died in Berlin, and who founded the philosophy of *identity* (the subject and object of thought exist as *identical* to one another in the Absolute; and intellectual intuition provides the path to recognition of this identity). He believed that nature is the same as mind, the same because nature and mind are created by the same Absolute. This creation resembles one great organism; nature is the visible spirit, and spirit (mind) is the invisible nature. Thus, they are identical. He revoked this philosophy towards the end of his life in favor of a more orthodox and religiously oriented system of thought. Key work: *The World Soul* (1897-99).

**Schiller, Ferdinand** (1864-1937). English philosopher who originally came from Ottensen, Germany. He taught at Oxford Univ. (1903-26), and later at the Univ. of Southern California (1929-36). He opposed the German (Hegelian)

151

idealism that reigned at Oxford in his time because it was too absolutist. He advocated instead a doctrine of *personal idealism,* or humanism, based on PROTAGORAS' formula that man is the measure of all things. He claimed that philosophy should address itself to the problems raised by the human struggle to comprehend the world of experience through the resources of the mind, and that dogmatic theorizing is an obstacle to man's quest. Key works: *Humanism* (1903); *Logic for Use* (1930).

**Schlegel, Friedrich von** (1772-1824). German philosopher who was born at Hanover and died at Dresden. He was the philosophical representative of German *romanticism,* a trend which sought a world different from the world of reality. Beginning as a rational liberal, he became disaffected with the potential of man and turned to more mystical pursuits. He concluded that the true object of philosophy is man's spiritual life and sought to develop a system totally devoid of science and the immediate evidence of reality.

**Schleiermacher, Friedrich Ernst** (1768-1834). German thinker who was born at Breslau and who developed a philosophy not unlike that of SCHELLING (the philosophy of *identity*) in that he claimed nature — the totality of existence — to be an organism. Through the unity of the real and ideal, truth — which resides with the Absolute as the ultimate unity — arises and is ever striven for by man. He used this philosophical world-view to construct a theory of religion. Key work: *On Belief* (1821).

**Schlick, Moritz** (1882-1936). German thinker, born at Berlin, who founded (1924) the Vienna Circle (a school of philosophy that emphasized a strict scientific approach to philosophical problems, using especially the logical analysis of language as its tool). He was an *empiricist;* his approach was based on his distinction between *experience* (which is immediate) and *knowledge* (which is the orderly organization of experience through concepts and language). He defined reality as all that which occurs in time. From this, he argued that the function of knowledge is to discover, isolate and interpret every *real* within the context of reality. This is done, he proposed, through scientific empiricism (examining the phenomena of experience through scientific methods of experimentation and observation). Key work: *Philosophy of Nature* (1934).

**Schopenhauer, Arthur** (1788-1860). Born at Danzig, and called the philosopher of *pessimism,* this German thinker based his work on the *critical idealism* of Kant. He believed that "the world is my idea of it," and felt that this statement is the primary fact of consciousness. But, he also claimed, the world is blind, obstinate, impetuous *will* (i.e. will in the sense of absolute cause of all things). As such, the world is one, while such things as time and space serve as principles of individuation, making the world intelligible to perception. This universal, one *will* generates everything in stages, through the self-objectification of ideas; indeed, the human will is an effect of the objectification of the *Universal Will.* The human will, too, is blind, obstinate and impetuous, and the only way of resisting its impulses is through the negation of all desire. Thus, man must live a life of negation. Key works: *The World as Will and Idea; Studies in Pessimism.*

**Schweitzer, Albert** (1875-1965). Born at Kaisersberg, Germany, he has become one of the universal geniuses of the 20th century — philosopher, historian, musician, physician, scholar, humanitarian, and an example for mankind. He renounced several promising careers early in his life to devote himself to medicine and to the caring and healing of the natives of Lambaréné in what was then French West Africa and is now the state of Gabon. His philosophy is as simple as it

153

is universal, and is based on a single concept — *reverence for life, all life*. All living creatures are worthy of sympathy, respect and love, regardless of race and color, regardless indeed of species or genus. He has advanced this philosophy especially in many of his later writings. Main works: *The Quest of the Historical Jesus* (1908); *Civilization and Ethics* (1929); *The Philosophy of Civilization* (1932).

**Seneca, Lucius Annaeus** (4 B. C.-65 A. D.). Born at Cordova, Spain, he became a Roman thinker who was at one time Nero's instructor but who fell out of grace and was forced to commit suicide. In his philosophy he emphasized the separation of soul and body, and is most noted for his advocacy of *stoicism*. He especially advanced a belief in the ethical principles of stoicism (virtue is the only good; the virtuous man is the man who has attained happiness through knowledge of himself and is independent of the external world). Key work: *Natural Questions*.

**Sextus Empiricus** (c. 200 A. D.). The writings of Sextus Empiricus are an arsenal of skepticism which has furnished pagan thinkers with weapons to combat Christianity, Christian apologists with arguments to refute paganism, and, in later centuries, philosophers like MONTAIGNE with reasons in defense of the independence of their minds on dogmatism of any kind.

Sextus, a physician by profession, was not so much an original thinker as an informed popularizer, a skilful and vigorous writer, who was able to summarize his thoughts by striking formulas. He attacked not only dogmatic philosophers and theologians but any expert, whether of mathematics or grammar, who claimed infallibility. In this way he has also given highly valuable information about the history of various sciences such as they had developed in his time.

**Shaftesbury, Third Earl of** (1671-1713). Born as Anthony Ashley Cooper in England, he was a pupil and later a patron of LOCKE, though in his own philosophy he opposed Locke's views. He advocated the so-called doctrine of *moral sense* (in man's nature there resides an innate sense of right and wrong which, rather than imposed moral theories, is the best guide to ethical conduct). Key work: *Inquiry Concerning Virtue or Merit* (1699).

**Shankara** (c. 825-875). He is considered by many Indian authorities to be the greatest Hindu philosopher. Reports of his life are adorned with myths and legends that ascribe to him superhuman powers and the performance of many miracles. He was revered as a saint and scholar, and his theoretical and practical teachings became of great consequence. He advocated the doctrine of *advarta* (i.e. the Absolute has a *personal* relation to the world; it is *absolutely* real, whereas the world and its individuals are only *relatively real*). As a result of this doctrine, his was basically a philosophy of devotion. He believed that devotion (in the sense of contemplation, not worship) is man's instrument of emancipation from ignorance and material enslavement. Although truth is to be understood intellectually, it is the highest spiritual intuition that leads to the union of the knower, the known, and knowledge. He often described the way to that goal as the denial of *selfness* in thought, feeling and action.

**Sidgwick, Henry** (1838-1901). A professor of philosophy at Cambridge Univ. and the last of the important English utilitarian thinkers, he was born at Skipton. Known principally for his work in ethics, he attempted to breathe new life into utilitarianism by sweeping away all hedonistic theories and infusing it with a morality of *common sense* (which held that some people outside of philosophy, with a great deal more experience in practical affairs than philosophers may have, are likely to have more common sense than philoso-

155

phers, and more instinct for what works best; hence, their experiences should be drawn upon by philosophers in rendering ethical theories). Key work: *Outlines of the History of Ethics* (1886).

**Siger de Brabant** (1235-1284). French philosopher who was a leader of medieval Averröism in Europe, against which AQUINAS argued on behalf of the Church. Proclaiming himself a "pure philosopher" (i.e. interested only in the non-religious aspects of philosophy), Siger chose the "truths of reason" over the "truths of faith", and advocated such doctrines as the eternity of the world, the unity of the human intellect, and the determination of all human affairs by the influence of the stars, all of which went directly against Catholic dogmas of creation, the individual soul, and divine providence. Key work: *On Generation* (1270); *Logical Questions* (1281).

**Simmel, Georg** (1858-1918). German philosopher who achieved great, if not lasting, fame during his later years. Born at Berlin, he taught at the Univ. of Berlin, then at Strassburg. He is remembered now for his development of a sociological philosophy and for his theory of *psychical relativism* (i.e. psychical interactions — as opposed to social interactions — between individuals are the basis for community life and the primary cause of social or community problems. Because of the psychological nature of relations between individuals, all ethical theories must be relative, taking into account the psychological considerations of human nature). Key work: *On Social Differentiation* (1890).

**Smith, Adam** (1723-1790). Though principally remembered as the author of *The Wealth of Nations* (1776), a classic in economic theory, this Scottish thinker also made significant contributions to moral philosophy and was long a professor of ethics and logic at the Univ. of Glasgow. The fundamentals of his ethical doctrine were centered in his doctrine of *moral sentiments* (i.e. sympathy is the basic constituent of moral awareness; hence the validity of any moral question should be judged by the measure of sympathetic response it evokes in the individual). Key work: *Theory of Moral Sentiments* (1759).

**Socrates** (c. 469-399 B. C.). Undoubtedly the most influential teacher of philosophy in ancient Greece, he lived in Athens practically all his life. Besides serving in the Athenian army, he also held several minor public offices. Because he eventually attained a secure financial position, he was able to teach without asking for fees. This, along with his refusal to submit to teaching official government doctrines when he felt they were contrary to good judgment, aroused the ire of both officialdom and his fellow teachers. He was accused of corrupting the youth of Athens, and was subsequently tried and sentenced to death. On several occasions he could have escaped from prison with the help of his many friends, but he insisted upon his obligation to respect the sentence, even though it was wrong. His justification for his own death, and his willing, philosophical acceptance of the poisonous hemlock that he felt it was his duty to drink, earned him the admiration of both his contemporaries and posterity. He is mainly known to history through the dialogues of PLATO, who was his student. His philosophy was based on his famous characterization of himself as an ignorant person whose only virtue was that he was aware of his ignorance. Rather than possess superficial knowledge, he would prefer to remain ignorant. However, his very knowledge of his ignorance compelled him to seek true knowledge. The road to such knowledge was via reason, and the result was virtue. According to him, then, virtue, which is embodied in knowledge, is the highest end of man. He left no written works.

**Soloviev, Vladimir** (1853-1900). The leading philosopher of religion in Tsarist Russia, he struggled against the alliance between the Orthodox Church and the state, insisting that by its nature the Church had a lust for power and that its political union only served to indulge and enflame that lust. He claimed that the Church lost its purpose by involving itself in the political realm. Deeply convinced of the truth of Christianity, he asserted the doctrine of *Godmanhood* (i.e. God and man working together without the mediation or intervention of the Church). Key works: *Crisis in Western Philosophy* (1874); *Justification of the Good* (1897).

**Sorel, Georges** (1847-1922). French social philosopher who saw in democratic political and social life the triumph of mediocrity. As a result, he espoused various forms of socialism, chiefly *syndicalism* (like anarchism, the belief that any form of government is an instrument of oppression and should be abolished; that productive and organized labor should be the ruling principle of society). His views had some influence on Italian fascism. Main work: *Reflections on Violence* (1908).

**Spencer, Herbert** (1820-1903). Born at Derby, England, and an engineer by training, he became one of England's foremost philosophers of *evolutionism*. His thought grew out of his intention to analyze and interpret life, mind, and society in terms of matter, motion, and force. He formulated a significant philosophical theory of evolution by comparing *evolution* to *dissolution*: dissolution is the *negation* of life, its very nature implying the disintegration of matter and the absorption of motion; on the other hand, evolution implies the *integration* of matter and the distribution of motion, and is the *affirmation* of life. Hence, the process of evolution, because of the impossibility of its opposite (dissolution), is the real life force. Main work: *System of Synthetic Philosophy* (1862-92).

**Spengler, Oswald** (1880-1936). Born at Blankenburg, Germany,

158

he was not a philosopher in the strict sense; however, in his book *The Decline of the West* (1918), he expounded a *philosophy of culture* that caused a great deal of philosophical controversy. The central thesis about which his doctrine revolves is that cultures, like individuals, develop to a certain point, then decline and eventually die; and that nations, or groups of nations, have an *inherent destiny* that cannot be changed or deflected by the efforts of mankind.

**Spinoza, Baruch** (1632-1677). One of the relatively few titans of philosophy, he was born at Amsterdam of a Jewish family that had been forced by religious persecution to flee Portugal. His early education in Amsterdam's Jewish community consisted principally of Biblical and Talmudic studies. Later he learned Latin, studied the natural sciences, and became particularly steeped in the philosophies of HOBBES and DESCARTES. While in his early twenties he began writing analytical treatises on the Bible that earned him the disapproval of the elders of the Jewish community. He was eventually banned (1656) and spent the rest of his life in relative isolation, for the most part studying and writing, while making his living as an optical lens grinder. Although his chief work is entitled *Ethics,* it could justifiably be called "Metaphysics", for it is a masterly metaphysical exposition of knowledge and is much more important for its original metaphysical insights than for its ethical conclusions. Using the mathematical method or argument developed by Descartes, he developed his entire philosophy around a conception of nature in which one, eternal, infinite *Substance* is the ultimate and immediate cause of all things (identical with the religious notion of God). This Substance is the self-caused, self-existing cause of nature, and pervades nature through and through. Thus, the only object of true knowledge is nature, for by knowing nature (in its cause), we know God. Arguing from this, he proceeded to relate Substance to the realm of individual beings. Although Substance is one and capable of no divi-

159

sion, it is also infinite and therefore is capable of having an infinite number of attributes (these being quite different than divisions). Of these infinite attributes, there are two (*thought* and *extension*) that are intelligible to man. It is by means of these two attributes that infinite Substance causes and penetrates nature and the finite world — although the two attributes themselves are infinite, they have an infinite number of *finite* modifications, of which man is one, and other things and beings in nature are others. Thus does Spinoza explain the cause of finite existence. Then, through the study and knowledge of the finite world (all nature), understood in all its ramifications as a manifestation of Substance (God), man is able to form an intellectual love of God which is the same as having a true knowledge of Him. Such a love demands disinterestedness and a complete liberation of the soul from corrupting or disturbing passions and emotions. The emotional balance created by such a state then enables man to live a virtuous ethical life, since lack of control over the emotions is the source of moral disintegration, and control is the source of moral perfection. Key works: *Ethics* (1677); *On the Improvement of the Mind* (1677).

**Spir, Afrikan** (1837-1890). A native of Russia (the Ukraine) who, after serving with distinction in the Russian navy, emigrated to Germany. His philosophy was strongly influenced by the analytical methods of SPINOZA and KANT. The main idea in his thought is that sensory experience and reasoning are contradictory, because the former keeps reminding us how things are *constantly in change* while the latter informs us of the *identity,* or basic *lack of change,* in all things. He tried to demonstrate the delusion of sense knowledge by showing that empirical data (the objects of sense knowledge) do not divulge the true nature of things. He claimed that only strict statements of fact — uncolored by emotional or sense interpretation — and strictly reasoned inferences from such statements could produce a real knowledge of things. Key work: *Thought and Reality* (1873).

**Steiner, Rudolph** (1861-1925). Born at Kraljevic, Croatia, this German theosopher started out on the path to a meaningful career as a philosopher of *evolutionary materialism* (of the sort that HAECKEL developed) when, at the age of 39, he underwent a complete personality change and plunged into a fanatical devotion to mysticism. He founded the Anthroposophical Society in Switzerland and turned from mysticism to the occult sciences. He claimed that his own moral purification and emancipation from egoistic drives enabled him to know realms of cosmic existence beyond the reach of the mortal mind. Key work: *On the Riddle of Man* (1916).

**Stern, Louis William** (1871-1938). Psychology-oriented, this German thinker, born at Berlin, developed new psychological methods of testing intelligence and invented the concept of the I. Q. (intelligence quotient) as a measure of intelligence. In philosophy, he was a *personalist*. He first demonstrated psychological differences of individuals, then contended that each person is a psychophysical unity unto himself; further, that all problems of knowledge and judgment should be understood through psychology. Key work: *Psychology and Personalism* (1917).

**Stevenson, Charles Leslie** (1908-   ). Born at Cincinnati, Ohio, and a professor of philosophy at the Univ. of Michigan, he is the leading American exponent of the *emotive theory* of ethics (i.e. in saying something is good, one automatically expresses one's approval of it based on an emotional reaction to it). One of his more significant conclusions, derived from the *emotive theory,* has to do with definitions: he argues that in many cases a definition is a disguised attempt to place the object or concept defined in a favorable or unfavorable light. Thus, all definitions should be rigorously

161

tested for objectivity before they are subscribed to. Key work: *Ethics and Language* (1944).

**Stirner, Max** (1806-1856). This was the pen name of Johann Caspar Schmidt, who was born at Bayreuth and espoused a thoroughly *individualistic* philosophy. He claimed that the *Ego* is the primary power of life and that all other divisions of existence must be subordinated to the individual, since it is in the individual that the life force (the Ego) is to be found. Whereas his contemporaries found the individual to be determined by collective factors of various kinds, Stirner proclaimed the absolute uniqueness and independence of the individual, insisting that the Ego is the only reality and is the sole value of existence. He was criticized severely for advocating a philosophy of selfish anarchy. Key work: *The Ego and His Own* (1845).

**Strauss, David Friedrich** (1808-1874). German religious philosopher whose fame derived principally from his controversial book, *Life of Jesus* (1838). He held that the unity of God and man is not realized in Christ, but in mankind itself and in its history. He believed this relation to be *immanent* (rooted in man's experience) rather than transcendental (rooted in God's experience).

**Suarez, Francisco** (1548-1617). A Jesuit priest, he was born at Granada, Spain, and was noteworthy as a political thinker whose views were quite independent and progressive for his time. He believed that the basis of all political authority was vested not in the will of monarchs but in the *sovereignty of the people,* while at the same time this authority came from God. Several European monarchs took this to be an attack on the doctrine of the divine right of kings and, as a result, banned his works. His views in philosophy and theology closely followed those of AQUINAS. Key work: *Metaphysical Disputations.*

**Swedenborg, Emanuel** (1688-1772). Swedish scientist, philosopher and theologian, his original name was Swedborg and he was born at Stockholm. After doing important work in mathematics and physics, he abandoned science and turned to mystical philosophy (1747). Central to his thought is his doctrine of *correspondence* (i.e. everything in the visible, natural, or material world *corresponds* to something in the invisible, spiritual world; the total natural world corresponds to the total spiritual world not only in general but in all particulars; thus, everything in the natural world is the representation of and corresponds to an idea in the spiritual world). According to this, man in the natural world is a representation of the idea of God in the spiritual world; it is through the rational comprehension of this idea that man can know God; however, such comprehension requires intense mystical communion. Key work: *Heavenly Secrets* (1749-56).

# T

**Tagore, Rabindranath** (1861-1941). Celebrated as the leading poet of India, he was also the respected author of philosophical works. After studying law in England, he returned to India and eventually founded (1901) a school, *Abode of Peace,* where students were educated in accordance with his principles. After the publication in English of his poems, he gained worldwide fame and was awarded the Nobel Prize (1913). He was knighted by the British government (1915). His philosophy is based on the belief in the progressive realization of the divine in man, and it shows little interest in supernatural destiny. He insisted that man's perfection will come in the world in which he is living. Key works: *Offerings* (1911); *Letters From Abroad* (1921).

**Taine, Hippolyte Adolphe** (1828-1893). French historian and thinker who was born at Vouziers and died in Paris. Markedly influenced by COMTE and MILL, he saw the essence of philosophy in discovering the underlying laws and principles of causality. He was a thoroughgoing *determinist* and held that man was a product of his heredity and environment. Key work: *On Intelligence* (1870).

**Tauler, Johannes** (1300-1361). German mystic philosopher and preacher who was born at Strassburg, Germany. He became a Dominican priest and studied at the Univ. of Cologne, where he was greatly influenced by the philosophy of ECK-

HARDT. His thought concentrated on a mystical form of ethics; he held that consciousness possesses the faculty of *analytical intuition* and that this intuition, contemplating immediate reality, could provide the means of grasping God. Key work: *Sermons.*

**Taylor, Alfred Edward** (1869-1945). Scottish philosopher who taught at Oxford before becoming professor of philosophy at the Univ. of Edinburgh. In his early years a Hegelian *idealist,* he later became steeped in Catholicism and a defender of the medieval Scholastic philosophy of the Church. His central doctrine is that God can be known to exist through the moral experience of man, which is to say that *conscience* is the common denominator of all theories of morality and is at the same time an imposed, rather than acquired, attribute of man. Hence, conscience affirms God because it is given by God. Key work: *The Problem of Conduct* (1901).

**Teichmüller, Gustav** (1832-1888). Born at Brunswick, Germany, and strongly influenced by LEIBNIZ and LOTZE, he taught a thoroughgoing *personalism* by regarding the "I", demonstrated and perceived directly through experience, as the real substance of life. He held that the moral world of ideas is a projection, or extension, of the determinations of the "I". He also held nature to be merely apparent, reality being given to it only insofar as the "I" relates to it via the ideas of the "I". The "I", of course, refers to the subject, or mind. Key work: *Studies in the History of Ideas* (1874).

**Telesio, Bernardino** (1509-1588). Italian scientific philosopher born at Cosenza, near Naples. He studied philosophy and mathematics at the Univ. of Padua; later in life he refused an appointment as archbishop by Pope Paul IV, choosing rather to devote his life to independent thought and scientific study. He founded and directed the *Academia Telesiana,* a school in Naples that propagated the scientific approach to knowledge and advanced the scientific movement in the Renaissance. His metaphysics envisioned man as a compound of the divine and the animal; he supported this view by examining man's psychic make-up and attempting to demonstrate that although man is divinely infused with soul, he also possesses psychical qualities that are shared by animal life. He concluded that man must be a combination of the natural and the divine. By taking this duality into consideration, it can then be said, according to him, that knowledge is founded upon sensation and memory, the former being a result of man's animal nature, the latter a result of his divine endowments. Key work: *On the Nature of Things* (1565).

**Temple, William** (1881-1944). Born at Exeter, he was a notable English philosopher of religion who for many years was an archbishop of the Anglican church. He held that the universe is made up of a series of levels of reality, with value as the highest level and directly intelligible through thought. Since God is the supreme value, He is ultimate reality. He was also a follower of MARX and an advocate of communist socialism. Key works: *The Nature of Personality* (1911); *Creative Mind* (1917).

**Tertullian, Quintus Septimus** (c. 160-240). A Roman thinker who converted to Christianity and became one of its most ardent apologists. He was untiring in expressing his contempt of non-Christian philosophers. To him, faith was above reason; any logical inquiry that raised contradictions was interpreted by him as merely an attempt to discredit Christian dogma; therefore, logic itself should be discredited. He introduced the concept of the Trinity (three persons in one God) into Christian thought. Toward the end of his life he himself became a heretic. Key work: *Apology.*

**Thales** (c. 625-545 B. C.). A native of Miletus in Asia Minor, he was the very first important philosopher of ancient Greece and was founder of the *Milesian* school of philosophy, the earliest trend of organized philosophy. His system was centered in his vision of the world as a manifestation and transformation of a single, cosmic, material substance — water. Although this concept was discredited by later Greek thinkers, his method of distinguishing between apparent nature and real nature by the unifying and relating powers of reason was of lasting consequence to philosophy.

**Theophrastus** (c. 372-287 B. C.). A pupil and successor of ARIS-TOTLE at the Lyceum in ancient Athens, he is important mainly for the work he did in refining some of the concepts of his teacher — he especially polished Aristotle's logical theory of syllogisms. He developed his own doctrines as well, the main one of which held that because the human intellect is immaterial, it is immortal.

**Thrasymachus** (c. 400-340 B. C.). Ancient Greek thinker who — like CALLICLES — advocated a philosophy of selfish aggressiveness. "Might," he said, "is right" — a motto that has characterized a particularly dangerous strain of philosophy throughout history. He criticized Plato's idea of justice (the adjustment of parts into a harmonious whole) by stating that justice is the province of the powerful and cannot endure the weak; therefore, he reasoned, the weak should be eliminated from earth in the interest of justice.

**Toland, John** (1670-1722). Born at Londonderry, Ireland, he was a significant religious philosopher, especially because his ideas were so contrary to the popular beliefs of his time. He declared that the true value of religion is not to be found in the supernatural, which is unintelligible to man, but in the natural and material world; and that in no sense can any part of truth be contrary to man's reason. Key work: *Christianity Not Mysterious* (1696).

**Trendelenburg, Friedrich Adolph** (1802-1872). German philosopher of idealism who restated the method and thought of HEGEL in terms of *motion* instead of dialectic. In other words, he felt that the cause of the world is to be found in the eternal, interacting movement of ideas, with a sort of Ultimate Idea (God) producing the motion. Key work: *Elements of Aristotle's Logic* (1836).

**Tufts, James Hayden** (1862-1942). American thinker. Born at Monson, Massachusetts, and a professor of philosophy at the Univ. of Chicago, he is principally remembered for his collaboration with DEWEY in the writing of the standard American sourcebook of pragmatic moral theory, *Ethics* (1908). His own ethical outlook had a strong sociological orientation.

**Turro y Darder, Ramon** (1854-1926). Born at Malgrat, Spain, he died at Barcelona. More important as a biologist than as a philosopher, he nevertheless contributed to the rebirth of philosophy in Spain at the beginning of this century. Using his biological discoveries as a base, he formulated a *dualistic* view of man as constituted of two essential, distinct, but cooperative, characteristics; *physiology* and *consciousness*. He claimed that these two basic traits were not merely related but were *conjoined* (man being unable to exist without both). Man likewise has two antagonistic conceptions of the universe — *objective* (from his physiological experience) and *subjective* (from the experiences of his consciousness). These two conceptions are synthesized by the necessary conjunctive action of his conjoined traits to produce a single, knowledgeable conception, which is the necessary starting point for further knowledge. Key work: *Critical Philosophy* (1919).

169

**Tzu Ssu** (c. 485-400 B. C.). Also known as Têng Shih, he was the grandson of CONFUCIUS and often evoked his ancestor's authority; but he also developed a philosophy of his own. Whereas Confucius had distinguished between true and supposed knowledge, he proceeded to speculations on the *relativity* of human knowledge of the universe; he held that the reality of the universe can be copied in the character of any wise man who is conscious of his moral and intellectual duty.

# U

**Unamuno y Jugo, Miguel de** (1864-1936). Born and raised at Bilbao, Spain, he became one of Spain's foremost philosophers and literary figures. After studying at the Central Univ. of Madrid, he became a professor of Greek at the Univ. of Salamanca (1891). He later became president of the school (1901). Philosophically, his thought was centered in his twofold conception of man — every man is an end in himself, and not a means to something else; however, man possesses a longing for immortality that is so much a part of his nature that it defies any attempts to remove it. Thus, man is a creature locked in an *eternal dilemma* — a completely natural being forever seeking a supernatural release. In trying to solve this dilemma, man finds no consolation in reason or intellect because reason and intellect are essentially dissolving forces. He must, then, rely on faith. But faith is something that requires conscious assent; it is an act of will. And will, by its very nature, requires reason and intellect. Since man cannot exist except within the horns of this dilemma, he must accept the opposition between faith and reason and try to cope with it. Because they are necessary conditions of human existence, they constantly interact and are interdependent. Being so, neither a purely religious nor a purely rationalistic doctrine is possible. This negative insight leads not to compromise, but creates instead a *tragic sense of life* and a tragic sense of history. Man, then, is essentially a tragic creature, constantly involved in an insoluble life situation. Main works: *Soliloquys and Conversations* (1910); *Against This and That* (1912); *The Tragic Feeling of Life in Men and Societies* (1914).

**Urakagina** (Date unknown). Probably in fact the world's first philosopher. He was one of the early kings of Babylonia, and as a thinker was almost exclusively concerned with ethics. In his ethical code (which was engraved in stone and discovered by archeologists), we find stated for the first time the universal principle that has been at the base of all the great moral systems of history — the *duty* of the strong to *protect* the weak.

# V

**Valentin** (c. 100-160). The leading Roman exponent of the philosophy of *gnosticism,* he was born at Alexandria, Egypt. He travelled to Rome (135) and taught there until his death. Dissatisfied with the common practice of speculating about God and His attributes, Valentin sought something higher and more complete which he called "gnosis" (a divine knowledge by which man could know God directly).

**Vaihinger, Hans** (1852-1933). Born at Nehren, Germany, he died at Halle. Strongly influenced by KANT, he developed a theory which he called the philosophy of "as if". This was based on his principle that reality cannot be known. Therefore, he argued, human beings construct systems of thought to satisfy their needs and then assume that reality agrees with their constructions. People act "as if" the real were what they assume it to be.

**Vico, Giovanni Battista** (1668-1744). Italian historical philosopher, he was born at Naples. After teaching for a number of years at the Univ. of Naples, he became official historian in the court of King Charles III. His chief contribution to philosophy consisted of his approach to the study of history, based on his *cyclical theory of history* which advanced the doctrine that history is a *spiral of progress* (i.e. humanity advances not in a straight line but in a circular, upward motion). In the *cyclical spiral* of development there is never any turning back to the original point of departure; every step and every turn is higher than the one before. Thus, according to Vico, history never repeats itself; what seems to man to be the repetition of history is merely a new view of an old landscape which, because we view it from a loftier position than before, enables us to see wider horizons. Finally, he declared that the end of history is freedom; hence, history is the process of the total liberation of human spirit, with each spiral bringing man closer to freedom (and therefore, it was implied, nearer to God, since the liberation of the spirit constitutes and is identical to participation in the divine). Key work: *Principles of a New Science* (1723-25).

**Volkelt, Johannes** (1848-1930). German thinker born in Galizia and mainly known for his highly original theory of knowledge. He held that knowledge has a dual source— (1) *empirical data* (since there can be no real knowledge of the external world without the process of the perception of externals); (2) *logical thought* (since it elaborates the crude intake of perception). Consequently, knowledge is the product of the rational mind operating on the materials of experience. From this, he postulated reality as *trans-subjective* (reality consists neither of mere objects nor of the refined perceptions of thought, but is rather a synthesis of both elements of existence). Key works: *Phenomenology and Metaphysics of Time* (1925); *Problem of Individuality* (1928).

**Voltaire, François Marie Arouet de** (1694-1778). Celebrated French historian, essayist, playwright and social critic, his contribution to philosophy was considerable, if indirect. As a philosopher of history he was one of the initiators of the modern history of civilization. A vigorous and aggressive *rationalist,* he scorned religion and insisted that man is capable of shaping the future of humanity in accordance with true (rational) morality by following the results of secular science and resisting the arbitrary authoritarianism and intolerance of religious morality. Key works: *Treatise on Metaphysics* (1734); *Discourse on Man* (1737); *Philosophical Dictionary.*

# W

**Wahl, Jean** (1888-    ). Born at Marseilles, this French philosopher and teacher coined the term "existentialism." He has made several important studies of the problem of existence and is, in fact, probably the founder of modern French *existentialism*. He is most noted for his *Treatise on Metaphysics* (1953), in which he advances the notion that a thread of contradiction runs throughout the history of philosophy. For Wahl, contradictory truths succeed themselves in time while at the same time they are in a state of simultaneous co-existence. Too, in every man there exists his own antithesis or contradiction, and it is this that leaves man in a state of indecision and, eventually, abandonment. Other key works: *Kierkegaardian Studies* (1938); *The Philosophies of Existence* (1954).

**Wang, Yang-Ming** (1472-1528). From Chokiang, China, he was influenced by Hindu as well as by Chinese thinkers and believed that philosophy should begin not with the investigation of the external world but with the examination of the inner self. He thus advocated the *psychic,* as opposed to the scientific or rationalist, approach to the mystery of nature.

**Wertheimer, Max** (1880-1943). Principally a psychologist, he was co-founder — with KOFFKA and KÖHLER — of *Gestalt Psychology* (the psychological analysis of knowledge that starts

**175**

from the assumption that the whole exists prior to its parts and is the only proper object of analysis). Born at Prague, Czechoslovakia, he taught and conducted experiments first at Frankfurt, Germany, then at the Univ. of Berlin. He claimed that phenomena must be considered as autonomous unities (coherent wholes), that the existence of each part of such a unity is dependent on the structure of the whole, and that knowledge of the whole cannot be derived from knowledge of its parts. This theory disrupted many important theories of knowledge. Key work: *Productive Thinking* (1943).

**Whewell, William** (1794-1866). An English philosopher, he was born at Lancaster and spent most of his life as a professor at Cambridge Univ. He pioneered the study of the *scientific method* of thinking, stressing the importance of induction in it. However, he regarded the "mysterious step" from the observation of particular facts to the discovery of general principles relating to them as dependent upon ideas formed by the "understanding" — that is, for the production of a scientific theory, the mere collection of facts is inadequate; what is required is "a true colligation of facts by means of an exact and appropriate conception." Based on this view, he developed what he called the *hypothetico-deductive* method — framing several tentative hypotheses and then selecting the right one. Although many of his ideas were attacked by MILL, his emphasis on the value of hypotheses in scientific thinking was a major contribution to philosophy. Key work: *Philosophy of the Inductive Sciences.*

**Whitehead, Alfred North** (1861-1947). An Anglo-American mathematical philosopher, he was born at Ramsgate, England, and died at Cambridge, Massachusetts. Taught mathematics and mechanics at the Universities of Cambridge (1911-14) and London (1914-24) before emigrating to the U. S., where he became a professor of philosophy at Harvard (1924-

38). He set out in his philosophy to rectify what he considered to be the great error in the philosophical tradition — the doctrine of the duality of reality (which held that reality is a compound of mind and matter). This "bifurcation of matter", as he called it, was initially posited by DESCARTES and, according to Whitehead, had poisoned philosophical thinking since. Whitehead claimed that there is only *one reality*: reality consists in only what appears, in what is perceived, in whatever is in the experience of a subject (subject meaning any actual entity). There are neither concepts nor substances in the world; only a network of events. All such events are actual extensions of the unified whole of the space-time relation. Hence, reality is based on the *patterned process of events*. He termed this world-view the philosophy of *organism*. From it he constructed a complex system of cause and effect, at the center of which is the concept of organisms in a kind of eternal relation within the framework of the space-time reality. Key works: *Principia Mathematica*, with RUSSELL, 3 vols. (1910-13); *Enquiry Concerning the Principles of Natural Knowledge* (1919); *The Concept of Nature* (1920); *Process and Reality* (1929).

**William of Champeaux** (1070-1121). French thinker, he was born at Champeaux and in his youth was a student of ROSCELIN. He later became a teacher of ABELARD. He was an extreme *realist* who believed that in every individual creature the entire species was represented in its totality.

**William of Ockham.** See OCKHAM, WILLIAM OF.

**Windelband, Wilhelm** (1848-1915). Born at Potsdam, Germany, he died at Heidelberg. Although the foremost German historian of philosophy of his time, his influence spread far beyond history. Using history as his frame of reference, he set out to effect a return to Kantian idealism, although an idealism much more reduced to essentials than that of KANT. He held that whereas it is for science to determine facts, it is for philosophy to determine values, or to be more exact, critical values. Facts may be gathered from experience, but values — or their corresponding judgments (what ought to be thought, felt and done) — cannot. They must be determined *a priori* (i.e. accepted as valid, though unproven by experience). From this he invented the doctrine of *normal conscience* (through whose criteria all critical judgments can validly be constructed). The existence of normal conscience established the existence of valid universal norms (similar to PLATO's Ideas) in which the *ideal norm* measures the value of each empirical fact or reality. The disciplines of logic, ethics and asthetics each have their system of universal norms, and it is these that render possible the true, the good and the beautiful. Main works: *History of Modern Philosophy* (1878-80); *Principles of Logic* (1914).

**Wittgenstein, Ludwig** (1889-1951). Austrian philosopher born in Vienna, he became a professor of philosophy in England at Cambridge Univ. (1928-51). Originally preoccupied with architecture, his *Tractatus Logico-Philosophicus* (1922) became of immediate consequence to philosophy and drew him permanently into philosophy. He contributed greatly to the development of logical positivism by offering a general means of removing philosophical difficulties by investigating the logical structure of language. He claimed that the inability to see through the logic of language is the cause of many apparently insoluble problems. Certain problems are stated incorrectly, or the language of their statements is not clearly understood, thus denying them the possibility of solution. He set up a system of *linguistic analysis* by which any statement must satisfy certain logical conditions before being admitted as a proper philosophical statement. The tools of his system are symbols, which enable a thing to be *shown* in the event that it cannot, because of the limitations of language, be *said*.

**Wolff, Christian** (1679-1754). A philosopher of the German Enlightenment, he was born at Breslau, taught at the Universities of Leipzig and Halle, and advocated *rationalism* to the fullest. Remembered mainly for his attempts to popularize philosophy by demonstrating the virtues of its logical and rationalistic foundations, he posited the world as a balance of good and evil and stated that it is incumbent upon man to transform evil into good to the best of his rational ability. He was banished from Germany for teaching the "atheistic" doctrine that man can be good without being a Christian.

**Woodbridge, Frederick J. E.** (1867-1940). Born in Canada, he became a significant American thinker who for many years was a professor of philosophy at Columbia Univ. An important member of the American *realist school* of thought, he conceived of reality as a twofold entity consisting of *structure* and *activity*. Structure determines what *can* exist, while activity determines what *does* exist. The relation between the two constitutes reality, while their interaction results in the *objectification* (realization, or bringing into actuality) of things. Since consciousness is a realization and derives directly from the relation, it is capable of understanding the relation, which, being the highest relation, is reality. Thus, the mind is capable of comprehending reality. Key work: *Nature and Mind* (1937).

**Wundt, Wilhelm** (1830-1920). German psychologist and philosopher who was born at Leipzig. After studying medicine at the Universities of Heidelberg and Berlin, he became professor of philosophy at the Univ. of Leipzig (1875), where he founded the first psychological laboratory (1879). He developed the science of *physiological psychology* by measuring in psychological terms physiological responses to stimuli. He then turned from his findings, which he felt constituted only a part of psychology, to the philosophical

179

analysis of psychical processes. He concluded that the *will*, together with the emotional states closely connected with it, is the basic element of psychological experience and is far more important than sensations or ideas. Key work: *Principles of Physiological Psychology* (1873-74).

# X

**Xenophanes** (c. 580-485 B. C.). Born at Colophon in Asia Minor, and usually associated with the *Milesian* school of ancient Greek philosophy, his main concern was in studying the phenomena of nature. He was the first of the Greek thinkers to advance the idea of One God. He phrased the celebrated saying: "The Gods of the Ethiopians are dark-skinned and snub-nosed; the gods of the Thracians are fair-skinned and blue-eyed; if oxen could paint, their gods would be oxen." This notion was a precursor of religious monotheism and philosophic pantheism.

**Xirau-Palau, Joaquin** (1895-    ). Born at Figueras, Spain, he later emigrated to Mexico. Specializing in philosophy, he received a Ph.D. from the Central Univ. of Madrid (1918), where he studied under ORTEGA Y GASSET. He insists that the very essence of thought opposes the conception of philosophy as a mere play of ideas or speculation of concept. The function of philosophy is to develop man in the sense of actualizing his inborn potentialities and bringing the fact and concept of personality into full fruition. The main characteristic of philosophy, then, according to him, is educational. Key work: *The Feeling of Truth* (1927).

# Y

**Yang Chou** (c. 440-360 B. C.). A great Taoist philosopher of ancient China whose teachings, along with those of Mo Tzu, strongly rivaled the Confucianist doctrines of Mencius. His principal teachings of following nature and preserving life have been distorted into purely *hedonistic* and *egoistic* doctrines by later Chinese commentators. However, he did teach that virtue is folly and that the concept of universal love is much inferior in its influence to *universal hatred*, which is the law of life. Key work: *Garden of Pleasure.*

**Yu-Lan Fung** (1895-   ). Author of the standard *History of Chinese Philosophy* (1930-33), he is not just a historian of philosophy but a creative and systematic thinker whose own philosophy of reality somewhat resembles that of Santayana, though it is thoroughly grounded in Confucianism. He distinguishes two realms of reality — that of *truth* and that of *actuality*. Reason belongs to the realm of truth; it is not in or above the world but is rather the regulating principle of everything that appears in the actual world. The realm of actuality is not created by reason, however; it is self-existent. Since reason merely regulates and cannot create, a principle that is neither in reason nor in the actual world is responsible for bringing things into real existence. This principle is called by him the *vital principle of the true prime unit.*

# Z

**Zeno of Elea** (c. 490-430 B. C.). A disciple of PARMENIDES in the *Eleatic* school of Greek philosophy, he invented *dialectics* and provided later Greek thinkers with models of logical argument. He defended the doctrine that only changeless being is real by means of indirect proofs showing the logical absurdities involved in the opposite view. Besides denying that plurality and change are real, he instituted a famous argument against the possibility of motion as the principal cause and explanation of all phenomena. He declared that motion was an illusion and could therefore not be the cause of things.

**Zeno the Stoic** (c. 340-270 B. C.). A native of the island of Cyprus, he founded the *Stoic* school of Greek philosophy at Athens. His thought was built on the principle that reality consists of a rational order in which nature is controlled by laws of reason. Men's lives are guided by a *Provident Reason* (much in the sense of God), against which it is futile to resist and to which the wise man willingly submits.

**Zoroaster** (c. 660 B. C.). Born in Persia, he was a religious leader and thinker who made many converts to his doctrines — until Zoroastrianism finally dominated Persia as a religion and spread throughout the Middle East. From his writings — the Avesta — which expressed his doctrines, it appears that he preached a form of *materialism* which later became similar to what we understand today as *vitalism*. There was a strong element of *dualism* in his mystical thought (i.e. good vs. evil), and it has been said that he was the first philosopher to establish the notions of *good* and *evil* as abstract values, as well as principles of nature.